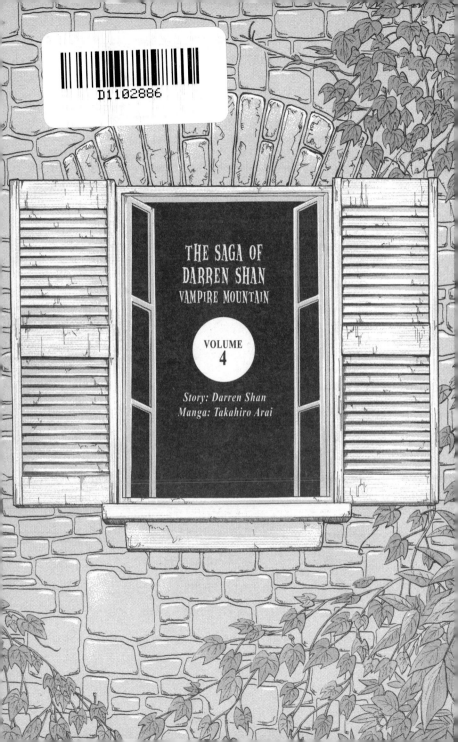

THE SAGA OF
DARREN SHAN
VAMPIRE MOUNTAIN

VOLUME
4

Story: Darren Shan
Manga: Takahiro Arai

A SUMMARY OF TUNNELS OF BLOOD:

DARREN AND EVRA SET OUT WITH MR. CREPSLEY, LEAVING THE SAFETY OF THE CIRQUE DU FREAK FOR MR. CREPSLEY'S HOMETOWN. DARREN ENJOYS HIS TIME THERE, ESPECIALLY WITH HIS NEW ROMANTIC INTEREST, DEBBIE, BUT EVERYTHING CHANGES WHEN A STRING OF GRISLY MURDERS EMERGES. THE SLAUGHTER COMES FROM THE CLAWS OF THE VICIOUS VAMPANEZE, MURLOUGH! WITH MR. CREPSLEY'S HELP, DARREN JUST BARELY SUCCEEDS IN STOPPING MURLOUGH, AND THE THREE HEAD BACK TO THE CIRQUE. TIME PASSES ONCE AGAIN...

VAMPIRE MOUNTAIN
CONTENTS

IT'S BEEN SIX YEARS SINCE WE LEFT MR. CREPSLEY'S HOME BEHIND AND RETURNED TO THE CIRQUE DU FREAK.

SIX PEACEFUL, HAPPY YEARS OF TRAVELLING THE WORLD WITH MY FELLOW PERFORM-ERS AND FRIENDS...

"MAYBE TOMORROW I'LL SHOW OFF THE NEW TRICK I'VE BEEN WORKING ON WITH MADAM OCTA...

"TODAY'S SHOW WAS ANOTHER SMASHING SUCCESS...

SHURU
(SLIDE)

SHURU

HEY, GET OFF!

"IN FACT, I COULD EVEN THROW IN THAT MAGIC TRICK MR. CREPSLEY TAUGHT ME..."

PATAN
(SLAM)

THAT SHOULD BE ENOUGH FOR TODAY'S DIARY ENTRY.

CHAPTER 25:
DESTINY LENDS
A HAND

DAR-REN.

PASA (FLAP)

WHAT IS IT, MR. CREPSLEY?

JA (GZSH) ミシ…

WE LEAVE FOR VAMPIRE MOUNTAIN TOMORROW.

PACK YOUR BAGS.

PLEASE BE READY AT DUSK.

I HAVE INFORMED MR. TALL OF THE PLAN.

THE COUNCIL ONLY MEETS ONCE EVERY TWELVE YEARS.

WE WILL PRESENT YOU TO THE COUNCIL OF VAMPIRE GENERALS.

HUH? VAMPIRE MOUNTAIN?

KARAN (K.CHNK)

GARA (CLANKS)

MUSHA

MUSHA (MUNCH)

MUSHA-(MUNCH)

SHAKA (CHAKA)

SHAKA

THESE GUYS EAT LIKE WILD PIGS! I DON'T THINK THEY HAVE ANY TASTE BUDS.

GARA (ROLL)

GARA

HOW IS IT, LEFTY? TASTES GOOD?

SFX: BAGU (MUNCH) HAGU

MY FRIEND EVRA IS A SNAKE-BOY.

ACTU- ALLY, BY NOW HE'S A SNAKE- MAN.

WE'RE STILL GOOD FRIENDS, BUT NOT EVERY- THING IS THE SAME AS BEFORE.

SAY, DARREN, CAN I HAVE SOME ADVICE?

I WANTED TO GIVE A CHRISTMAS PRESENT TO THAT GIRL I FANCY...

WHAT SHOULD I GET HER?

AS A HALF- VAMPIRE, I AGE AT ONE- FIFTH THE REGULAR RATE.

EVRA'S GROWING INTO A MAN, BUT I'VE STILL GOT THE BODY OF A KID.

I ALWAYS KNEW THIS WOULD HAPPEN EVENTU- ALLY...

...BUT I'D BE LYING IF I SAID I WASN'T SAD ABOUT IT.

YEAH, APPARENTLY I'VE GOT TO BE PRESENT FOR THIS VAMPIRE COUNCIL.

THAT'S REALLY COMING OUT OF THE BLUE.

YOU'RE LEAVING FOR VAMPIRE MOUNTAIN *TONIGHT*?

YOU'LL BE CLIMBING TREACHEROUS MOUNTAIN PATHS AND DEALING WITH THE SNOW AND COLD.

FROM WHAT I KNOW, THE JOURNEY TO VAMPIRE MOUNTAIN'S NO JOKE.

YOU NEARLY DIED SIX YEARS AGO. I DON'T WANT TO BE RESPONSIBLE FOR YOU AGAIN.

STAY HERE AND HAVE A WONDERFUL CHRISTMAS WITH YOUR GIRLFRIEND.

HUH?

MAYBE I SHOULD GO WITH YOU!

EVRA...

IT'LL BE LIKE THE TIME WE LEFT FOR CHRISTMAS, SIX YEARS AGO!

GASA GOGO (RUSTLE)

LET'S SEE, BOOTS, JACKET ...

WELL, I GUESS THAT'S TRUE. I'D PROBABLY FALL ASLEEP AND HIBERNATE TILL SPRING!

HA HA HA!

SPEAK-ING OF "COLD," I THOUGHT SNAKES DIDN'T LIKE IT!

HEY, DON'T BE COLD, DARREN ...

HANG ON, I DON'T NEED *THIS*, DO I?

DARREN...

IT'S QUITE PORT-ABLE, SO GREAT FOR LONG TRIPS.

MR. CREPSLEY GOT THAT FROM SOMEONE NAMED EVANNA, YEARS AGO.

PEKO (POP)

WELL, THIS FOLDING STEW POT LOOKS LIKE IT SHOULD BE USEFUL.

!!!

EVERYONE KNOWS THAT VAMPIRES THRIVE ON DANGER!

CHIKKU (TICK)

WHY, OF COURSE HE DOES!

BUT VAM-PIRES ARE GREAT CLIMB-ERS.

YOU'RE *REALLY* GONNA NEED THIS ROPE!

CHIKKU

CHIKKU

I KNOW, BUT DO YOU REALLY WANT TO HANG OFF THE SIDE OF A MOUNTAIN WITH ONLY YOUR FINGERTIPS FOR SUPPORT?

ズ゛ (ZUZU) ズ゛ (ZUZU) ズズ (ZUZU) ZUZU ZUZU (ZW000) ZUZU ZUZU ズ゛ (ZUZU)

GOOD TO SEE YOU AGAIN TOO, MR. TINY...

GU... (GRAB)

グ゛ (GU)

CAN IT REALLY BE SEVEN YEARS ALREADY?

I CAN'T TELL YOU HOW MANY VAMPIRES I KNOW WHO DIED BY BRAVING THE SUN ON A DARE!

YOUNG MASTER SHAN.

THEY *LOVE* A CHALLENGE.

VAMPIRES ARE PECULIAR CREATURES.

HIS CLOCK, HIS LOOKS, THE EVIL HE EXUDES... MR. "DESTINY."

I COULD *NEVER* FORGET HIM.

YOU REMEMBER ME! I'M HONOURED.

SU (SHH)

BURU (SHIVER)

BURU

BIKU (TWITCH)

WE MEET AGAIN, EVRA VON.

THANKS FOR YOUR HELP WITH MY LITTLE PEOPLE.

THE WINDS THAT GUST AROUND VAMPIRE MOUNTAIN WOULD CUT EVEN A TOUGH-SKINNED YOUNG MAN LIKE YOU TO THE BONE.

THE WAY IS LONG, AND THE NIGHTS ARE COLD.

I WOULD ADVISE YOU TO TAKE MATCHES, MASTER SHAN.

SO, YOU'RE OFF TO THE WILDS OF VAMPIRE MOUNTAIN.

THANKS FOR THE ADVICE.

MORE RELAXING THAN ANY LULLABY...

OH, THE DELIGHTFUL SCREAMS!

I TELL YOU, YOU SHOULD HAVE SEEN THAT EARTHQUAKE!

AH, LARTEN! PROMPT AS EVER. HAVE A SEAT.

HERE I AM.

GACHA (CLICK)

NO, DESMOND...

THANK YOU, BUT I WILL STAND.

WE LEAVE TONIGHT.

I HEAR YOU'RE TAKING OFF FOR VAMPIRE MOUNTAIN.

FU (CHEH)

IT IS NOT EASY.

THE PATH TO VAMPIRE MOUNTAIN IS AS HAZARDOUS AS EVER, ISN'T IT?

YOU ARE WELL IN-FORMED.

THIS IS THE FIRST COUNCIL YOU'VE BEEN TO IN ABOUT FIFTY YEARS, ISN'T IT?

DARREN CAN LOOK AFTER HIMSELF.

DANGER-OUS FOR A YOUNG SNIP OF A THING LIKE MAS-TER SHAN, WOULDN'T YOU SAY?

YES...

I'M SURE HE CAN, BUT IT'S UNUSUAL FOR ONE SO YOUNG TO MAKE THE JOURNEY, ISN'T IT?

KOKU (NOD)

CHIRA (FLICK)

MY LITTLE PEOPLE SHOULD COME IN QUITE HANDY.

THAT'S WHY I'M SENDING THESE TWO ALONG AS GUARDS.

ZUZU (SHUFFLE)

MY LITTLE PEOPLE?

IN THE WAY?

THEY WOULD GET IN THE WAY. I DO NOT WANT THEM!

GUARDS?

LEFTY!

NEVERTHELESS, I DO NOT WANT...

THEY'LL BE LIKE SHEPHERDS, WATCHING OVER THE TWO OF YOU WHILE YOU SLEEP.

THEY EXIST ONLY TO SERVE!

AND WHEN WE GET THERE?

YOU WILL NOT BE RESPONSIBLE FOR THEIR FOOD AND BEDS.

ALL YOU HAVE TO DO IS MAKE SURE YOU DON'T "LOSE" THEM IN THE SNOW ALONG THE WAY.

THEY'RE GOING WITH YOU. END OF STORY.

THIS IS NOT AN *OFFER.*

LISTEN.

DON'T FORGET BY WHOSE HANDS THE HALL OF PRINCES WAS BUILT.

THEY KNOW WHICH SIDE THEIR BLOOD IS BUTTERED ON.

DO YOU EXPECT ME TO TAKE THEM INSIDE VAMPIRE MOUNTAIN?

THE PRINCES WILL NOT STAND FOR IT!

I *KNEW* YOU'D SEE IT MY WAY!

KOKU (NOD)

YOUR BATTLES WITH THE WOLF-MAN AND MURLOUGH HAVE TOUGHENED YOU.

THAT'S WHERE IT *REALLY* MATTERS.

YOU'VE GROWN, MY BOY. ON THE INSIDE, I MEAN.

NOW, MASTER SHAN...

H-HOW DO YOU KNOW ABOUT MURLOUGH...?

BE STRONG AND KEEP FAITH IN YOURSELF.

YOU MUST BE STRONG, DARREN. STRONG!

GI (CREAK)

I KNOW *EVERY-THING*.

ZU SU (SHH)

...BUT THERE'S A LONG WAY YET TO GO.

YOU'VE COME A LONG WAY...

...EVEN WHEN IT SEEMS INEVITABLE.

NEVER ADMIT DEFEAT...

WE'LL MEET AGAIN, I'M SURE.

I'LL BE ON MY WAY...

WE'VE ALL GOT PLACES TO BE AND DEADLINES TO MEET.

TIME'S TICKING...

HA (GASP)

THAT'S ALL I HAVE TO SAY.

ZU SU

OF COURSE I AM.

YOU'RE NOT BRINGING *HER*, ARE YOU?

HUH?

WHERE IS MADAM OCTA?

GOGO (RUSTLE)

GREAT. I BET I KNOW WHO GETS TO LOOK AFTER HER...

ALL RIGHT, THEN.

THERE IS SOMEONE ON VAMPIRE MOUNTAIN I WISH TO SHOW HER TO.

ZAZAAN (SPLASH!!)

MOZO (RUSTLE)

GET READY FOR ONE LONG, HARD TRIP.

DID YOU HEAR ALL THAT, MADAM?

READY?

THANKS, EVRA. I'LL NEED IT!

TAKE CARE, DARREN. WE'RE ALL WISHING YOU LUCK.

...WE CLEARED THE CAMP, LET THE TWO SILENT LITTLE PEOPLE FALL INTO PLACE BEHIND US...

LEAVING THE SAFETY OF THE VAN...

READY.

GOGOOH (DOOMMMM)

...AND SET OFF ON WHAT PROVED TO BE A PERILOUS, DEADLY ADVENTURE...

...INTO LANDS COLD AND FOREIGN AND STEEPED IN BLOOD.

VAMPIRES PLACE MUCH WEIGHT ON PRIDE AND NOBILITY.

WE CAN'T BE LATE TO THE COUNCIL, BUT WE CAN'T FLIT EITHER. THERE ARE MANY RULES AND CUSTOMS TO FOLLOW.

I'VE LONG SINCE LOST TRACK OF TIME.

WE'VE BEEN TRAVELLING FOR THREE WEEKS... OR IS IT MONTHS? I DON'T KNOW.

THE LAND AROUND US IS BARREN AS FAR AS THE EYE CAN SEE.

YOU CAN HARDLY SPOT A SINGLE ANIMAL, MUCH LESS PEOPLE.

CHAPTER 26:
STREAK

LIFE IS A CHALLENGE TO A VAMPIRE. ONLY THOSE WHO RISE TO THE CHALLENGE TRULY KNOW WHAT IT MEANS TO LIVE.

AT LEAST THAT'S WHAT MR. CREPSLEY SAYS.

HAA (CHUFF)

HAA

HE TOLD ME MANY THINGS ON THE ROAD.

THERE WERE OVER A MILLION VAMPIRES ONCE, BUT NOW THEY HAVE DWINDLED TO TWO OR THREE THOUSAND, AND ONLY THREE TO FOUR HUNDRED OF THEM ARE GENERALS.

IN COMPARISON, THERE ARE AROUND TWO TO THREE HUNDRED VAMPANEZE.

BYOOOOOOSHHH
(WHOOOOOOSHHH)

THE LONG, COLD TREK HAS WORN ME DOWN.

ARE YOU MANAGING, DARREN?

HAA
HAA
(CHUFF)

THE LITTLE PEOPLE FOLLOW, SILENT AND ALOOF.

AND IT'S AGAINST THE RULES TO SAVE A WEAKER VAMPIRE.

I KNOW WE CAN'T BE LATE TO THE COUNCIL.

OUR BOTTLES OF BLOOD ARE FOR EMERGENCIES ONLY, SO WE CONSERVE WHEN POSSIBLE.

WE ONLY TAKE ANIMAL BLOOD SPARINGLY, AND HUMAN BLOOD EVEN LESS.

I THINK YOU ARE STARTING TO UNDERSTAND THE VAMPIRE WAY.

HA HA...

YEAH, I'M FINE.

MR...
CREPS...
LEY...

......

HAA !!?!

HAA !!?!

SFX: KURA (SWOON)

GARA GGS HUNK

I WILL SLOW THE PACE A TAD...DO NOT FALL BEHIND.

I KNOW.

PARA PARA (PATTER)

GA (SNAG)

AAAH!!

DARREN!!

GAVNER PURL IS THE VAMPIRE GENERAL WHO TOLD MR. CREPSLEY ABOUT MURLOUGH, SIX YEARS AGO.

GAV-NER PURL!

DARREN SHAN!

WELL, WELL! LOOK WHO IT IS!

APPARENTLY, HE FOLLOWED MR. CREPSLEY'S AURA TO FIND US HERE.

GOHHHHH (WHOOOOSHH)

HANG IN THERE, BOYS! WE'RE NEARLY TO THE WAY STATION!

WITH GAVNER IN TOW, WE MOVED ON INTO SNOWDRIFTS, BLIZZARDS AND WORSE...

THERE WILL BE COFFINS AND BOTTLES OF BLOOD THERE!

A PLACE TO STOP AND REST!

WAY STATION?

THERE IT IS, STRAIGHT AHEAD!

THE WAY STATIONS WERE INTRODUCED AFTER OUR WAR WITH THE VAMPANEZE, WHEN OUR NUMBERS DWINDLED.

SOME VAMPIRES OBJECT TO THEM AND NEVER USE THEM, BUT MOST ACCEPT THEM.

WE CAN REST AND RECOVER HERE FOR A WHILE.

HUH? WHY...?

STAY CLOSE BEHIND ME, DARREN.

MU CHMMD

YES.

GAVNER...

... *VAMPIRE* BLOOD!

IT IS A FEW DAYS OLD...

BLOOD? WHOSE IS IT?

IT TASTES LIKE...

PERO (CLICK)

THAT IS UNLIKELY, BUT POSSIBLE. UNFORTU- NATELY, THIS MAKES IT UNWISE TO SPEND ANY TIME HERE.

IT WAS PROBABLY THE WORK OF A WILD BEAST. BUT IT *MIGHT* HAVE BEEN A VAMPIRE HUNTER...

ONE OF OUR CLAN WAS KILLED HERE.

AGREED. WE'LL HAVE TO PROCEED WITH CAUTION.

PER- HAPS I SHOULD ...

DARREN IS NOT A CHILD. HE WILL BE FINE.

I'LL CIRCLE BACK TO THAT STREAM TO FILL THE CAN- TEENS.

WHAT IF THAT HUNTER OR BEAST CATCHES SCENT OF YOU?

ALL BY YOUR- SELF?

WE SHALL CAMP UNDER HERE.

THE LIGHT WILL SOON RETURN.

BE BACK IN A BLINK!

JABA (SLOSH)

JABA

BRRR... IT'S FREEZ- ING.

TO (TEK)

A WOLF!?

GURURURU
(GRRRR)

OH, NO!

BA
(LEAP)

COULD HE BE WHAT SPILLED THAT BLOOD EARLIER?

GOKU
(GULP)

!!!

GAAA
(RAHHH)

......

......!

PERO
(CLICK)

PERO
(CLICK)

PERO

!!

GASA
(RUSTLE)

GASA

UOOOON
(AWOOOO)

HA
HA
(PANT)

A FINE SPECIMEN! A BORN LEADER.

LEGENDS CLAIM THAT ONCE, OUR SPECIES CAME FROM THE SAME ROOT.

COUS-INS?

I SEE YOU HAVE MET SOME OF OUR COUSINS, DARREN.

THERE THERE

AHH.

WOLVES AND VAM-PIRES ARE KINDRED SPIRITS, YOU SEE!

DON'T BE A SPOIL-SPORT!

YOU NAMED THEM? THEY ARE WOLVES, NOT DOGS.

AND THIS LITTLE PUP IS RUDI, AS IN RUDOLPH THE RED-NOSED REINDEER!

SEE HIS RED NOSE?

GUESS WHAT! I'VE DECIDED TO CALL HIM "STREAK."

SEE HOW HE HAS THIS STREAK OF BLACK HAIR ON HIS BELLY?

I SUP-POSE NOT...

IT CAN'T DO ANY HARM.

LET HIM GIVE THEM NAMES IF HE WANTS.

IT'S SO WARM ...

A H H ...

IT WAS THE FIRST TIME I HAD A GOOD DAY'S SLEEP IN AGES.

MORE?

DID YOU SEE ANY MORE OF THEM, DARREN?

-JI- (STARE)

NO NEED TO GLARE, LITTLE ONE.

WHAT A PARADE WE MAKE!

VAMPIRES, HALF-VAMPIRES, WOLVES, AND LITTLE PEOPLE...

SO STREAK AND HIS PACK ARE HEADED FOR THE SAME DESTINATION!

IT'S AS IF THERE'S A WOLF COUNCIL GOING ON AT THE SAME TIME!

HA HA

THEY KNOW FROM EXPERIENCE THAT THERE WILL BE PLENTY OF SCRAPS FOR THEM TO FEED ON.

WOLVES COME WHENEVER THERE'S A COUNCIL.

THIS IS TROUBLE.

AW, GREAT...

WE CANNOT AVOID THAT.

IT'LL BE CHILLY, THOUGH!

NO, IT WOULD TAKE TOO LONG.

HOW ABOUT WE GO AROUND?

DAAAAHH!!

BA

BA (MMF)

SFX: BURU (SHIVER) BURU

BEST TO KEEP THEM INTACT, SEE.

OUR CLOTHES WOULD PROTECT US A LITTLE, BUT WE'D COME OUT THE OTHER END IN TATTERED RAGS.

WHAT ARE YOU GETTING UNDRESSED FOR?

WOW, IT'S FREEZING!

W-WHAT ARE *THOSE*?

...WERE A PRESENT.

THEY, UH...

PAOON (PAWOOO!)

WHAT!

BRISK NIGHT FOR IT!

ZURU (SLIP)

PFFT!

HEH HEH

...SHE JUST HAD VERY BAD TASTE IN UNDERWEAR.

SHE WAS A BEAUTIFUL WOMAN...

FU (CHEH)

HA HA!

AND IN BOYFRIENDS, I'D SAY.

BFFT!

AAH-HA

HA HA

VAM-
PANEZE
BLOOD!!

WHAT'S UP?

IT IS CLEAR...

CAN YOU SMELL IT, UP AHEAD?

VAMPANEZE ON THE PATH TO VAMPIRE MOUNTAIN? IT'S COMPLETELY UNHEARD OF!

THAT'S CRAZY!

IT MAY HAVE SOME RELATION TO THAT VAMPIRE BLOOD.

BUT VAM-PANEZE, IN *THIS* AREA?

PIN (TING)

GAVNER AND I WILL CONDUCT THE SEARCH.

YOU WAIT WITH THE OTHERS BEHIND THAT OUTCROPPING.

AGREED!

WHATEVER THE REASON, IT IS CLEAR WE MUST SCOUT THE AREA.

YOUR
SHARP
NOSE
WILL BE
A GREAT
BOON.

WILL
YOU
COME
ALONG?

KUI...
(TUG)

KUI

I HOPE
THEY'RE
ALL RIGHT
...

LET'S
FIND SOME
FOOD FOR
WHEN THEY
GET BACK!

GOOD
IDEA!

YOU
MIGHT
NOT
GET
DOWN!

DON'T
GO
TOO
HIGH,
RUDI!

CHAPTER 27:
HARKAT SPEAKS!

TH-THAT'S THE BIGGEST BEAR I'VE EVER SEEN IN MY LIFE!!

...BUT I CAN'T LEAVE RUDI BEHIND TO FEND FOR HIMSELF!

I COULD ESCAPE ON MY OWN...

COME ON, GRIZZLY!!

GABU (CHOMP)

GA (SNARL)

DO

SUTA (STOMP)

GUJAA
(GRSHHK)

JIWA....
(SPLUT)

GUN
(HRRG)

GA
(SNAG)

NO,
LEFTY!

BA
(WHUP)

GATA (SHIVER)

AAH... AAH...

GATA

BIKU

BIKUN (TWITCH)

I WOULD HAVE BEEN A GONER IF YOU HADN'T STEPPED IN.

THANKS FOR COMING TO MY RESCUE.

PERO (LICK)

PERO

SU (SHG)

D A R R E N !!

IT ATTACKED ME OUT OF NO-WHERE...

WHOA! WHAT THE BLAZES HAPPENED HERE?

ZUBA (SLASH)

AND IF YOU DID NOTHING TO UPSET IT...

IT MAKES NO SENSE. BEARS DO NOT BEHAVE SO AGGRESSIVELY IN THIS MANNER.

SHA (SHKK)

I WILL HAVE TO EXAMINE IT CLOSER.

...BUT NOT WITH RABIES.

AS I SUSPECTED...THE BEAR *WAS* INSANE...

WELL?

KUN (SNIFF)

VAMPANEZE!?

IT HAD CONSUMED THE BLOOD OF A VAMPANEZE!

WE MUST SEARCH THE AREA.

THE BLOOD OF VAMPIRES AND VAMPANEZE IS POISONOUS.

WELL, IF THIS WAS THE OWNER OF THAT BLOOD IN THE TRAIL OF THORNS, WE DON'T HAVE TO WORRY ABOUT HIM ANYMORE.

SO THE BEAR DUG THIS BODY UP AND ATE PART OF IT...

BUT BURIED BY **WHOM?**

JUST LOOK...

THE BODY HAS CLEARLY BEEN BURIED.

WORRY? QUITE THE CON-TRARY.

THIS IS **MORE** WORRY-ING.

?

YOU TOO DID WELL. LEFTY, IS IT?

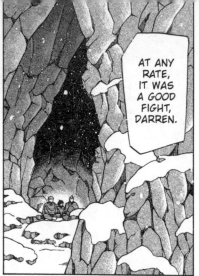

AT ANY RATE, IT WAS A GOOD FIGHT, DARREN.

I AM SORRY ABOUT YOUR PARTNER...

IT SEEMS WE WERE RIGHT IN BRINGING YOU ALONG.

!!!

PASA (FLAP)

GUI (TUG)

N...

KAPA (THWUP)

HAR-KAT...

HARKAT... MULDS...

NAME... NOT LEFTY...

...TALKED...

HE...

FIRST... I AM A GHOST...

I WILL TELL YOU... WHAT I... REMEMBER...

MY MEMORIES... ARE NOT... COMPLETE.

NI...NIKO (G-GRIND)

MUCH IS... CLOUDED.

SFX: PECHI (SCRITCH) PECHI

...I... WAS A GHOST.

WHAT I SHOULD... HAVE SAID IS...

AIN'T YA?

HARDEST GHOST I'VE EVER SEEN!

MR. TINY HAS THAT MUCH POWER? TO BRING BACK THE DEAD?

KOKU (NOD)

SFX: ZEH (WHEEZE) / HAA (HUFF)

suu (SSK)

suu

BUT WHAT-EVER DEAL...I MADE...AND MY MEMORIES...OF LIFE...

...ARE ALL...GONE.

I MADE A DEAL...WITH MR. TINY...AND RECEIVED THIS...BODY.

WITH-OUT IT...I WOULD DIE WITHIN...TEN HOURS.

I MUST BREATHE...THROUGH ITS FILTERS...AND CHEMICALS...TO SURVIVE.

YOUR MASK...

NOT SURE...BUT DON'T...THINK SO.

COULD YOU AGREE TO ANOTHER CONTRACT WITH MR. TINY?

ONE SHOT AT...EXTRA LIFE IS...ALL I THINK...WE GET.

HOW CAN YOU DIE IF YOU'RE ALREADY DEAD?

IF IT DOES...MY SOUL GOES...

...BACK TO THE WAY...IT WAS.

MY BODY CAN...DIE, LIKE ANY-ONE'S.

WHY HAVE *YOU* BROKEN THAT LONG SILENCE, HARKAT? AND *WHY*?

IN ALL THE HUNDREDS OF YEARS THAT WE HAVE KNOWN THEM, NO LITTLE PERSON HAS EVER SPOKEN.

...I MEAN, HARKAT...

WELL, LEFTY...

I HAD NO... CAUSE TO.

THE LITTLE PEOPLE...CAN READ EACH... OTHER'S MINDS.

...WHY DIDN'T YOU EVER SPEAK BE-FORE?

IT IS FOR... PRINCES... NOT FOR... YOUR EARS.

A *MES-SAGE*? WHAT SORT?

MR. TINY... GAVE ME IT...TO GIVE TO... VAMPIRE PRINCES.

I HAVE A... MESSAGE...

BUT...

GO ON, HARKAT.

WE WON'T TELL THEM YOU TOLD US. WILL WE, DARREN?

SO I'D... HAVE TO... SPEAK... SOON ANYWAY.

BURU
(SHIVER)

BURU

YOU
WILL...
NOT
TELL?

......

PLEASE,
HARKAT.

I WANT TO
KNOW TOO.
WHAT MESSAGE
DID MR. TINY
LEAVE WITH
YOU?

MY
LIPS
ARE
SEALED.

I
PROMISE.

VERY...
WELL...

HAA
(SIGH)

...THAT...

...VAMPIRE
PRINCES...

GOKURI
(GULP)

MR.
TINY
TOLD...

...ME
TO
TELL
...

......?

...NIGHT OF THE... VAMPANEZE LORD...IS AT HAND.

VAMPANEZE LORD? WHAT'S THAT?

GAVNER? MR. CREP-SLEY?

GATA

GATA

GATA (SHIVER)

...OF THE TRUE TERROR THOSE WORDS SHOULD HAVE INSPIRED WITHIN ME.

AT THE TIME I HAD NO IDEA...

THE NIGHT OF THE VAMPANEZE LORD IS AT HAND!

...THAT GAVNER FINALLY DECIDED TO TELL THE TALE.

IT WASN'T UNTIL A FEW NIGHTS LATER...

MR. CREPSLEY AND GAVNER COULDN'T EXPLAIN THE MESSAGE RIGHT AWAY.

WHAT COULD HARKAT'S WORDS HAVE MEANT?

HE SAYS, "VAMPANEZE HAVE NO HIERARCHY."

MR. TINY, HE DELIVERS A MESSAGE TO THE VAMPIRES.

IT ALL STARTS 700 YEARS AGO, WHEN THE VAMPANEZE DECIDED TO BREAK AWAY FROM THE VAMPIRES.

NO GENERALS OR PRINCES.

NOBODY GIVES ORDERS AND NOBODY TAKES THEM.

HIERARCHY?

...I AGREE WITH SOME OF THAT.

AND TO BE HONEST...

...WAS THE VAMPIRE GENERALS AND PRINCES.

YOU SEE, DARREN, ONE OF THE REASONS THE VAMPANEZE BROKE AWAY...

......

THEY DIDN'T LIKE THAT A FEW VAMPIRES COULD ORDER THE MAJORITY AROUND LIKE THEY DO.

I JUST HAPPEN TO THINK *SOME* OF THEIR IDEAS ARE WORTH TAKING ON BOARD.

...BUT IT'S NOT LIKE I WANT TO BE A VAMPANEZE IN THE SLIGHTEST.

SUU
SUU
(ZZZ)

NOW I'M SURE LARTEN WOULD HAVE WORDS WITH ME ABOUT THIS...

MR. TINY, HE TELLS THE VAMPIRE PRINCES...

OH, RIGHT, RIGHT!

WHAT MR. TINY TOLD THE PRINCES...

WHAT WAS I TALKING ABOUT, AGAIN?

BUT LISTEN TO ME RAMBLE.

"ONE NIGHT, A CHAMPION WILL STEP BEFORE THE LEADERLESS VAMPANEZE."

"...AND THE OTHER VAMPANEZE WILL FOLLOW HIM BLINDLY AND DO EVERYTHING HE SAYS."

"HE WILL BE KNOWN AS THE VAMPANEZE LORD..."

...THAT WE VAMPIRES CANNOT WIN.

PA (TOSS)

IT IS A WAR, ACCORDING TO MR. TINY...

AND WHEN HE COMES TO POWER, HE WILL LEAD THE VAMPANEZE IN ANOTHER WAR AGAINST THE VAMPIRES...

PACHI (POP)

PACHI

DARREN, HAVE YOU EVER *MET* MR. TINY?

IS IT TRUE? DOES HE KNOW THAT?

IT'S HIS ABILITY TO READ THE FUTURE...

CHI

CHI STIK?

...HIS FORE-SIGHT.

SCARE ME? IT FELT LIKE HE WOULD KILL ME AND EAT ME...

BUT THAT'S NOT THE SCARIEST THING ABOUT HIM.

HA HA, TOO TRUE!

DID HE SCARE YOU?

Y-YEAH, JUST TWICE...

EVERYTHING THAT HAPPENED 700 YEARS AGO, FROM THE VAMPANEZE INDEPENDENCE TO THE TRUCE THAT FOLLOWED...

...HAPPENED EXACTLY AS MR. TINY HAD PROPHESIED BEFORE THEY OCCURRED.

BUT IT'S DANGEROUS TO TAKE HIS EVERY WORD AS TRUTH.

HE'S BEEN KNOWN TO LIE FROM TIME TO TIME...

...HE'S AN EVIL LITTLE WORM.

AS YOU KNOW...

SO IF THE VAMPANEZE LORD DOES INDEED APPEAR, THE VAMPIRES WILL HAVE TO FIGHT?

EXACTLY. IT WOULD MEAN MR. TINY WAS TELLING THE TRUTH AFTER ALL...

WHAT'S THAT?

YOU'LL SEE WHEN WE GET TO VAMPIRE MOUNTAIN.

THE STONE OF BLOOD.

HA (PANT)

HA

THERE'S ONE HOPE, THOUGH.

HOPE?

...AND PROSPER ONCE AGAIN.

MR. TINY SAID THAT IF WE PREVENT IT FROM FALLING INTO THE HANDS OF THE VAMPANEZE...

...LONG AFTER THE BATTLE HAS BEEN FOUGHT AND LOST...

...THERE'S A CHANCE THAT VAMPIRES MIGHT RISE FROM THE ASHES...

LET ME KNOW IF YOU FIGURE IT OUT!

SFX: PACHI (WINK)

THAT'S ONE THAT HAS PUZZLED US EVER SINCE WE HEARD IT.

HOW WILL THAT HAPPEN?

VAM-PANEZE LORD...

STONE OF BLOOD...

GAA

GUAA (SNRR)

THAT WAS FAST

UH, GAVNER...

GORON (ROLL)

NOW LET'S GET SOME SLEEP.

WE'RE NEARLY AT VAMPIRE MOUNTAIN.

HA HA

GAAA (SNORR)

GAAA

WHOA...

BUT FINALLY, VAMPIRE MOUNTAIN WAS BEFORE OUR EYES ...

HOW MANY MOUNTAINS, VALLEYS, NIGHTS DID WE CROSS TO GET THERE?

WHAT'S SO FUNNY?

HEH HEH ...

BWA HA HA HA HA!

WHERE'S THE PALACE?

WHERE THE VAMPIRE PRINCES LIVE.

DO NOT GET LEFT BEHIND!

THE MOUNTAIN'S A GIANT HIVE OF CAVES AND CHAMBERS!

RIGHT!

BA (LEAP)

ZUSA (ZSHH)

HOW LONG DO YOU THINK WE WOULD ESCAPE DETECTION IF WE BUILT A PALACE ON THE SIDE OF A MOUNTAIN?

THEN WHERE...?

IT'S *INSIDE* THE MOUNTAIN!

OH, I BET I KNOW!

FUN (CHMPLD)

UOON (AWOOO)

PIN (TING)

GOOO (WHOOOSH)

HE IS SAYING GOOD-BYE.

HERE? DO THEY HAVE TO GO?

WHAT IS IT, STREAK?

HA HA (PANT)

UOOON

NICE KNOWING YOU, STREAK ...

GYU (SQUEEZE)

IT WOULD BE CRUEL TO ASK THEM TO STAY WITH US.

THEY CAME TO MEET OTHERS OF THEIR KIND.

I'LL MISS YOU, RUDI, YOU MISERABLE LITTLE RUNT ...

I-I'LL BE OKAY. THEY'RE JUST A PACK OF DUMB OLD WOLVES. I DON'T CARE.

YOU'LL SEE HIM AGAIN.

WE'LL LOOK THEM UP WHEN WE LEAVE.

KOHON (AHEM)

MANGY!?

COME. WE CANNOT STAND HERE ALL NIGHT, PINING OVER A FEW MANGY WOLVES.

SFX: GIRO (GLARE)

THAT'S THE SPIRIT.

......

...REALLY?

THE CUB WILL REMEMBER YOU EVEN WHEN IT IS OLD AND GREY.

YOU KNOW, DARREN, WOLVES NEVER FORGET A FACE.

YES.

UOOON
(AWOOO)

UOU
(AWOO)

UOU

SEE YOU AGAIN SOME-DAY!!

TA TA
(TEK)

BYOOO
(WHOOOSH)

KARA
(CRUMBLE)

KARA

GASHA
(KSHRK)

WHERE'S
THAT
FAINT
LIGHT
COMING
FROM?

GOOO
(FWSHHH)

SOUNDS
LIKE
WATER...
A RIVER?

IT'S A
FORM OF
FUNGUS
THAT GIVES
OFF LIGHT.
IT GROWS
HERE AND
THERE IN
THE
MOUNTAIN.

...COME
AGAIN?

LUMI-
NOUS
LICHEN.

KASASA
(SCUTTLE)

LOOK! I'VE NEVER SEEN A SPIDER LIKE THAT BEFORE!!

WHAT'S WRONG!?

WHOA!

O-OKAY!

DON'T WANDER OFF, DARREN. THIS PLACE CAN BE A MAZE.

WE MUST MAKE HASTE, LEST WE ARRIVE TO THE COUNCIL LATE.

SUCH SPIDERS CAN BE FOUND ALL OVER THIS MOUNTAIN. IT IS NOT RARE IN THE LEAST.

WASHA

WASHA
(SNIK)

GOKI
(CRIK)

WOW...

GOOD. WE APPEAR TO HAVE MADE IT IN TIME.

I AM GAVNER PURL...

I AM LARTEN CREPSLEY...

...COME TO SEEK COUNCIL.

MMM.

...COME TO SEEK C-COUNCIL!

I-I AM DARREN SHAN...

MU
(HMPH)

BUT...

LARTEN CREPSLEY AND GAVNER PURL ARE RECOGNIZED BY THE GATE.

CHA
(CHK)

COME... SEEK COUNCIL.

I... HARKAT MULDS.

...THESE OTHER TWO...

DO YOU VOUCH FOR HIM?

THE BOY IS MY ASSISTANT, A HALF-VAMPIRE.

THEY ARE OUR TRAVELLING COMPANIONS.

BA
(WHOOSH)

THEN DARREN SHAN IS RECOGNIZED BY THE GATE.

I DO.

YOU LIE! I THOUGHT THE LITTLE PEOPLE COULDN'T SPEAK...

HIS NAME IS HARKAT MULDS. HE IS A LITTLE PERSON ...

WHAT BUSINESS HAS HE AT COUNCIL?

BUT *THIS* IS NO VAMPIRE!

HARKAT HAS A MESSAGE FOR THE PRINCES, TO BE DELIVERED IN PERSON.

WE ALL DID. BUT THIS ONE CAN.

WHAT!?

A MESSAGE FROM DESMOND TINY...

ENTER AND FARE WELL!

ZA (STOMP)

THE HALLS ARE OPEN TO ALL OF YOU!

H-HARKAT MULDS IS RECOG-NIZED BY THE GATE!

BI (ZWAP)

...AND OUR LONG, LONG JOURNEY TO THE HALLS OF VAMPIRE MOUNTAIN...

...WAS AT AN END.

THIS IS A HALL OF WELCOME. THE HALL OF OSCA VELM!

WE'RE FINALLY HERE, DARREN!

CHAPTER 29:
QUARTERMASTER SEBA NILE

YES. MOST OF THE HALLS OF VAMPIRE MOUNTAIN ARE NAMED AFTER FAMOUS VAMPIRES.

IS OSCA VELM SOMEONE'S NAME?

SHOES?

DOSSARI (STUFFED)

PICK OUT A PAIR OF SHOES, DARREN.

WHEW! THAT WAS SOME TRIP.

TON (TAP)

TON

HARKAT MULDS (LITTLE PERSON)... EVEN MY NAME.

THEY'RE CARVING THE NAMES OF EVERYONE WHO'S ATTENDING THE COUNCIL.

KAN

KAN (CLANG)

GAVNER PURL, LARTEN CREPSLEY...

JA (ZSH)

AREN'T YOU HUNGRY?

EAT UP, DARREN!

SFX: HYOI (CHOMP)

ZUI (CHRMPH)

DOSASA (SPILL)

PUHAA (AHHH)

NO, YOU DRINK STRAIGHT FROM THE JUG! LIKE THIS!

AREN'T THERE ANY CUPS?

WATER!

WINE!

DON (WHAM)

BLOOD!

DODON (WHAM)

BWA HA HA HA

GEHO (COUGH)

ゲホ

ゲホ

GEHO

ブッ

GOKU (GULP)

HITA (SPLISH)

BAT BROTH DOES NOT AGREE WITH ME.

NO BROTH FOR YOU?

モグ MOGU (CHEW)

モグ MOGU

THE *BEST!*

GA (MUNCH)

GA

THIS IS GREAT!

CHAPU (FLOAT)

チャプ

OF COURSE. WHAT DID YOU *THINK* IT WAS MADE OF?

THIS IS *BAT* BROTH!?

WHAT TOOK YOU SO LONG?

SEBA!

I HAVE OFTEN SEARCHED FOR YOU MENTALLY, IN THE HOPE THAT YOU WERE NEAR!

HA HA!

GASHI (HUG)

IT HAS BEEN A LONG TIME, OLD FRIEND!

THIS IS HARKAT MULDS.

AND IS THAT... A LITTLE PERSON?

WELCOME, GAVNER PURL.

BEEN A WHILE, SEBA!

WHEN I SENSED YOU COMING, I HARDLY DARED BELIEVE IT!

PON (PAT)

PON

GREETINGS, HARKAT MULDS.

I HAVE NOT SEEN ONE OF THOSE SINCE MR. TINY VISITED US WHEN I WAS A BOY.

A LITTLE PERSON... AND WITH A NAME, NO LESS.

PACHI (BLINK)

PACHI

HELLO...

I WAS JUST AS SURPRISED THE FIRST TIME I HEARD HIM SPEAK.

HE *TALKS*?

A PLEASURE, SIR.

GATA (TWITCH)

...MY ASSIS- TANT.

AND THIS IS DARREN SHAN...

I KNOW.

YOU, LARTEN— WITH AN ASSISTANT?

GREET- INGS, DARREN SHAN.

GU (SHAKE)

......

THE PRINCES WILL NOT APPROVE... AND SO YOUNG.

MOST PROBABLY NOT...

...AND WILL GET THE BETTER OF THOSE WHO TRY AND BEST HIM.

DO NOT LET HIS AGE FOOL YOU— HE IS AS SLY, CUNNING AND QUICK AS ANY VAMPIRE...

...THE QUARTER-MASTER OF VAMPIRE MOUNTAIN.

DARREN, HARKAT! THIS IS SEBA NILE...

...AND REPLACE IT WITH A LESSER VINTAGE.

YOU ONCE TRIED TO STEAL HALF A VAT OF MY FINEST WINE...

DO YOU REMEMBER, LARTEN?

AS YOU KNOW FROM EXPERIENCE.

AND WHAT HAPPENED?

WAKU CHEE WAKU

I WAS YOUNG AND FOOLISH. THERE IS NO NEED TO REMIND ME...

NIYA GRIND

I HAD SWALLOWED HALF A BOTTLE BEFORE I REALIZED.

HE EMPTIED THE VAT AND REPLACED THE WINE WITH VINEGAR.

WELL... SEBA GOT TO THE WINE FIRST.

GUBI (GULP)

GI (CREAK)

TELL HIM, LARTEN.

DARREN!

......

HA (CHA) HA HA HA

I WAS YOUNG. I DID NOT KNOW BETTER.

NO! *YOU* OF ALL PEOPLE, LARTEN?

OEEE (BLAARGH)

I SPENT THE REST OF THE NIGHT RETCHING.

I SEE NOW...

I LEARNED MOST OF WHAT I KNOW AT HIS HANDS.

SEBA WAS MY MENTOR.

HO HO

INDEED YOU DID.

BUT I TAUGHT YOU, LARTEN, DID I NOT?

I NEVER REALLY THOUGHT ABOUT THE FACT THAT MR. CREPSLEY WOULD HAVE BEEN YOUNG ONCE...

A TIME WHEN HE WAS SEBA'S PUPIL...

UTO (BLINK)

IT'S A STRANGE... FEELING...

HA HA HA HA HA

AND NOW, MR. CREPSLEY IS MY MASTER...

SUUU (ZZZ)

HA (GASP)

DARREN, ARE YOU ALL RIGHT?

DAR-REN...

COME ALONG, DARREN.

WE WILL TALK MORE TOMOR-ROW.

GATA (THUMP)

COME, I WILL FIND ROOMS FOR YOU.

HE HAS NEVER MADE THE JOURNEY BEFORE.

HA-HA, THE BOY IS TIRED.

...BUT IN TIME YOU WILL GROW ACCUSTOMED TO THE PLACE.

FOR THE FIRST FEW NIGHTS YOU MAY FEEL LOST...

AND THIS IS THE HALL OF RUKA DI PRIATORE.

YOU MIGHT CALL IT A HOSPITAL.

ZO (SHIVER)

THIS IS THE HALL OF FLAVIO KAPELLO.

WE STORE WEAPONS HERE.

IT IS THE QUARTERMASTER'S DUTY TO SEE THAT EVERY PERSON WHO VISITS VAMPIRE MOUNTAIN...

...IS PROVIDED WITH EVERY AMENITY.

INCREDIBLE! AND YOU REMEMBER EVERY SINGLE ROOM?

SEPARATE! I HAD ENOUGH OF GAVNER'S SNORING ON THE TRAIL.

I'D TAKE THE BIG...

OR SEPARATE QUARTERS?

WOULD YOU PREFER ONE BIG ROOM FOR THE GROUP?

HA HA...

HE'S GOT A WAY WITH WORDS, DARREN.

CHARMING!

THAT'S FINE...BY ME.

THAT'S NOT TRUE!

VERY WELL.

AFRAID TO SLEEP BY YOUR-SELF?

OH?

HARKAT AND ME DON'T MIND DOUBLING UP, I THINK ...

THIS ROOM SHOULD SUIT YOU.

I DID TOO, WHEN I WAS YOUR AGE. IT WAS A GOOD GUESS.

WAIT! HOW DID YOU KNOW I LIKE HAM-MOCKS?

I'M... NOT A FAN OF COF-FINS.

WOULD YOU PRE-FER A HAM-MOCK?

COF-FINS, HUH?

WAIT, SEBA. I HAVE SOMETHING TO SHOW YOU.

THANK YOU!

I WILL SEND ONE FOR YOU TOMORROW. I LOOK AFTER MY GUESTS!

TAKE A LOOK.

RIGHT AWAY, SIR.

DARREN, FETCH MADAM OCTA.

MY GOOD-NESS...

MOZO (RUSTLE)

OH, LARTEN! WHAT A BEAUTY!

IT IS ALL RIGHT, DARREN. SEBA KNOWS WHAT HE IS DOING.

STOP! DON'T LET HER OUT—SHE'S POISONOUS!

PAKA (PLOP)

I HAVE NEVER SEEN SUCH A SPIDER...

GASA (SKITTER) GASA (SKITTER)

PURAAN
(DANGLE)

SHE IS MARVEL-LOUS!

ア二

ZAZA
(ZSHH)

KASA
(SCUTTLE)

KASA

KASA

I THOUGHT I KNEW OF ALL THE SPIDERS IN EXISTENCE, BUT THIS ONE IS NEW TO ME...

FU
(CHEH)

FU

INCREDIBLE! I ALWAYS HAVE TO PLAY THE FLUTE...

...CONCEN-TRATING WITH ALL MY MIGHT TO MAKE SURE SHE DOESN'T BITE ME...

I WISH TO MAKE YOU A PRESENT OF HER.

I THOUGHT YOU WOULD LIKE HER. THAT IS WHY I BROUGHT HER.

SU (SSK)

YOU MUST TELL ME MORE ABOUT HER WHEN YOU GET THE CHANCE.

PAA (GLOW)

FOR YOU, OLD FRIEND— ANYTHING.

YOU WOULD PART WITH SUCH A WONDERFUL SPIDER?

I DO NOT HAVE THE TIME TO CARE FOR SUCH AN EXOTIC PET...

I AM KEPT BUSY TRYING TO KEEP UP WITH JOBS I ONCE ZIPPED THROUGH.

I MUST REFUSE...I AM OLD AND NOT AS SPRIGHTLY AS I USED TO BE.

AYE. I WOULD LOVE TO TAKE HER, BUT I CANNOT. I KNOW MY LIMITS.

....

ARE YOU SURE?

I WILL.

ONLY THE YOUNG HAVE THE ENERGY TO TEND TO THE NEEDS OF SPIDERS OF SUCH CALIBRE.

LOOK AFTER HER, DARREN— SHE IS BEAUTIFUL AND RARE.

UNTIL WE MEET AGAIN.

NOW, I MUST GO.

PASA (FLAP)

GOOD NIGHT, GAVNER, MR. CREPSLEY.

SLEEP, AND REGAIN YOUR STAMINA.

GOOD-NIGHT, DARREN!

ENOUGH! I AM NOT MOPING!

COME ON... DON'T LET IT GET YOU DOWN!

BUCK UP!

MOZO

MOZO (WRIGGLE)

UNTIL... THEN.

IN THAT CASE, SEE YOU TONIGHT.

NO. BUT I CAN SLEEP...ON FLOOR.

CAN YOU FIT IN THE CASKET, HARKAT?

GORO (ROLL)

TONIGHT?

NO WAY TO TELL IF IT'S MORNING OR NIGHT DOWN HERE...

IT COULD BE TOMORROW MORNING, FOR ALL I KNOW...

BETWEEN THE EXHAUSTION OF MY TRIP AND THE EXCITEMENT OF REACHING VAMPIRE MOUNTAIN, MY MIND WAS IN DISARRAY...

...BUT BEFORE I KNEW IT, I HAD FORGOTTEN EVEN THAT I WAS LYING IN A CASKET AND PLUNGED INTO A DEEP, DEEP SLEEP...

SIGH... FINALLY MADE IT TO VAMPIRE MOUNTAIN...

I WONDER WHAT THE COUNCIL WILL... BE... LIKE...

CHAPTER 30:
THE LIFE OF A VAMPIRE

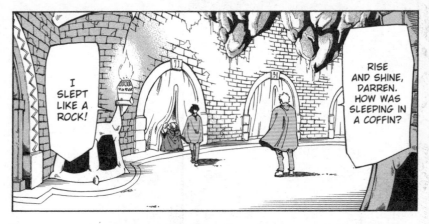

RISE AND SHINE, DARREN. HOW WAS SLEEPING IN A COFFIN?

I SLEPT LIKE A ROCK!

READY FOR MORE BAT BROTH, THEN?

LARTEN AND SEBA ARE ALREADY EATING.

I'D SAY WE'RE STARV- ING!

RIGHT, HAR- KAT?

GOOOO (WHOOOSH)

NEED TO USE THIS FIRST?

WHAT DOES "WC" MEAN?

WC

WATER CLOSET. DON'T FALL IN!

?

HI (CHEE)
ヒヒ

94

GOHHH

POKKARI
(PLOP)

GII
(CREAK)

WHAT'S THAT NOISE?

ZUZAA
(ZSHHH)

WE CALL IT THE HALL OF KHLEDON LURT.

HERE'S THE MEAL HALL!

GAYA (MURMUR)

GAYA

ALL THE TOILETS ARE BUILT RIGHT OVER THEM!

YES. THERE ARE A COUPLE OF BIG STREAMS LEADING OUT OF THE MOUNTAIN.

WHAT WAS *THAT?* ARE ALL THE TOILETS LIKE THAT?

KHLEDON WAS A GENERAL OF GREAT STANDING. IN THE WAR OF VAMPANEZE INDEPENDENCE...

...HE DIED IN THE ACT OF SAVING THE LIVES OF MANY OTHER VAMPIRES.

PRETTY COOL, HUH?

SFX: MUXHA (MUNCH) / HAGU (CHEW)

GA (CHOMP)

GA

GAYA

GAYA (MURMUR)

IT'S AMAZING TO LOOK AROUND AND REALIZE THAT EVERY ONE OF THESE PEOPLE...

...IS A VAMPIRE!

I'LL SEE YOU AGAIN LATER, HARKAT.

SO WE'LL BE GOING NOW. ENJOY YOUR-SELVES!

SEE YOU... LATER.

GATA (THUMP)

I'VE GOT TO GO TO THE HALL OF PRINCES. WILL YOU ACCOMPANY ME, HARKAT?

YES. WE OUGHT TO REPORT MR. TINY'S MESSAGE, THE DEAD VAMPANEZE, AND THE RUINED WAY STATION AS WELL.

TO PRES-ENT YOUR-SELF?

WAI

WAI (CRAHH)

GAYA

GAYA

WE PUSH OURSELVES TO THE LIMIT, AND WOULD RATHER FACE DEATH ON OUR FEET THAN LET OUR FRIENDS LOOK AFTER US IN OLD AGE.

VAMPIRES LIVE HARD, TESTING LIVES.

UH, I WAS JUST NOTICING THAT IT SEEMS TO BE ALL MEN HERE... AND HARDLY ANY OF THEM ARE OLD.

WHAT IS IT, DAR-REN?

SEVEN HUN-DRED !?

HARDLY ANY OF THEM MAKE IT TO 700 YEARS OLD, AS I HAVE.

VERY FEW VAMPIRES LIVE TO BE A RIPE, OLD AGE.

HIS OPEN CURIOSITY IS REFRESHING. YOU WERE THAT WAY ONCE TOO.

PEACE, LARTEN. DO NOT CHASTISE THE BOY.

DARREN!

GATA (THUMP)

HOW COME YOU'VE LIVED SO LONG THEN?

I WOULD RATHER HAVE DIED YOUNG IN BATTLE, BUT WE SERVE AS WE MUST.

I HAVE NO CHANCE TO PARTAKE IN FIGHTING OR HUNTING... BUT IT IS AN HONOURABLE PROFESSION.

BEING QUARTER-MASTER MEANS LIVING INSIDE VAMPIRE MOUNTAIN FOR THE REST OF MY LIFE.

I HAVE SURVIVED THIS LONG BECAUSE OF MY POSITION, DARREN.

ACCEPT DARREN'S QUESTIONS AND STUBBORNNESS.

...BUT YOU HAVE MUCH TO LEARN ABOUT TEACHING.

YOU ARE A VAMPIRE OF VERY GOOD STANDING, LARTEN...

A MAN GROWS TIRED OF LIFE WHEN HE HAS LIVED SO MUCH OF IT...

IT IS JUST OUR WAY.

IT SEEMS CRAZY TO ME. WHY DO YOU PUSH YOURSELVES SO HARD?

THAT IS ENOUGH, LARTEN.

DO NOT TALK BACK, DARREN!

BUT...

YOU SEE, LARTEN, STUDENTS NEVER APPRECIATE THEIR TEACHERS WHILE THEY ARE LEARNING.

GOOD TEACHERS EXPECT NO PRAISE OR LOVE FROM THE YOUNG.

IT IS ONLY LATER, WHEN THEY KNOW MORE OF THE WORLD, THAT THEY UNDERSTAND HOW INDEBTED THEY ARE TO THOSE WHO INSTRUCTED THEM.

THEY WAIT FOR IT, AND IN TIME, IT COMES.

YES, I AM.

NIYA (SMIRK)
ニヤ…

ARE YOU SCOLDING ME, SEBA?

THANK YOU, DAR-REN.

MY PLEASURE, LARTEN.

WOULD YOU PASS ME A LOAF OF BREAD?

オホン (AHEM)

YOU CALL THESE SHOWERS?

I'LL FREEZE! THIS IS TORTURE!

WHAT DO YOU THINK OF OUR SHOWERS, DARREN?

MOST OTHER VAMPIRES RARELY VENTURE HERE TO THE HALL OF PERTA VIN-GRAHL!

BUT IT IS THE ONLY SHOWER TO BE FOUND IN VAMPIRE MOUNTAIN! YOU WILL HAVE TO BEAR IT!

ZAZAA (ZLOSHH)

HA HA!

BRACING? FELT MORE LIKE MURDER TO ME...

NOW THAT WAS BRACING!

IT SURE WAS INTERESTING, THOUGH!

POKA (PUFF)

POKA

BUT THE FIRST HALLS WERE NOT BUILT UNTIL 1,400 YEARS AGO. THAT IS WHEN THE FIRST PRINCES MOVED IN AND THE COUNCILS BEGAN.

ZAWA

ZAWA (MURMUR)

THIS MOUNTAIN WAS FIRST USED BY VAMPIRES AROUND 3,000 YEARS AGO.

KILL THEM ALL!

CURSED VAM-PANEZE...

MR. TINY'S MESSAGE IS ALREADY GETTING AROUND...

THE NIGHT OF THE VAMPANEZE LORD...

DID YOU HEAR THE NEWS?

...BUT YOU MAY HAVE YOUR PICK.

THE CLOTHES HERE MAY BE TOO BIG TO FIT YOU WELL...

ANOTHER RED CAPE... HE REALLY LIKES HIS RED.

BASA (FLAP)

SEBA WEARS RED TOO...

NOT JUST HIS WAY OF DRESSING, BUT ALSO HIS WAY OF SPEAKING.

HA HA.

AS YOU WILL HAVE NOTICED, I HAVE COPIED MANY OF SEBA'S WAYS.

BATAN (SLAM)

HAA (CHUFF)

HAA

IT IS A MEASURE OF THE RESPECT I FEEL FOR HIM...

BA (WHAM)

NO!!!

IS THAT YOU, KURDA?

OH... THAT'S DIFFERENT.

IT IS GOOD TO SEE YOU, OLD FRIEND.

YES.

...

... LARTEN?

AND THIS IS...?

MY NAME IS DARREN SHAN.

THE ONE I'VE BEEN HEARING ABOUT!

I'M KURDA SMAHLT. IT'S A PLEASURE TO MEET YOU, YOUNG ONE!

THEY SEEM FAMILIAR...

THREE SCARS ON HIS LEFT CHEEK...

QUESTIONS. AS SOON AS THAT MESSAGE FROM MR. TINY CIRCULATED, EVERYONE RAN TO **ME** TO ASK IF IT WAS TRUE.

WHAT WERE YOU RUNNING FROM?

I DID NOT SAY THAT.

YOU DON'T APPROVE.

GAVNER PURL TOLD ME ABOUT YOUR INVESTITURE. CONGRATULATIONS.

IT'S NOT SUCH A BIG DEAL. IT'S NOT LIKE I'VE DONE ANYTHING WONDROUS.

WHEN ONE MOVES UP IN THE ORGANIZATION.

WHAT'S AN INVESTITURE?

HOW *DO* YOU BECOME A VAMPIRE PRINCE?

THAT'S RIGHT. I'M BEING MADE A PRINCE.

UNLIKE THE PROCESS TO BECOMING A GENERAL...

...THERE'S NO FIXED WAY TO BE A PRINCE.

JUST CURIOUS.

N-NO!

THINKING OF APPLYING FOR THE JOB?

WHY THE INTEREST?

USUALLY A PRINCE IS SOMEONE WHO'S DISTINGUISHED HIMSELF IN MANY BATTLES, EARNING THE TRUST AND ADMIRATION OF HIS COLLEAGUES.

TO BE A GENERAL, YOU STUDY A SET NUMBER OF YEARS AND PASS REGULAR TESTS.

...AND I ONLY BARELY SQUEEZED IN BY THE VOTE.

NI (GRIND)

ONE OF THE PRINCES OBJECTED TO MY NOMINATION...

ONE OF THE ESTABLISHED PRINCES NOMINATES HIM. IF THE OTHER PRINCES AGREE, HE'S AUTOMATICALLY ELEVATED UP THE RANKS.

OK

OK OK

IF ONE OBJECTS, THE GENERALS VOTE AND THE MAJORITY DECISION DECIDES HIS FATE.

NO

OK OK

VOTE

WHICH MEANS THAT NEAR ENOUGH ONE IN TWO THINK I WON'T!

JUST FIFTY-FOUR PERCENT OF THE GENERALS THINK I'LL MAKE A FITTING PRINCE.

IF TWO OR MORE PRINCES OBJECT, THE MOTION'S REJECTED.

NO

OK NO

COME NOW, DON'T LEAVE THE BOY THINKING IT'S MY *AGE* THEY OBJECT TO.

KURDA IS ONLY 120 YEARS OLD, MAKING HIM ONE OF THE YOUNGEST PRINCES EVER...

...AND MANY GENERALS BELIEVE HE IS TOO YOUNG TO COMMAND THEIR RESPECT.

THE PRINCES HAVE ALWAYS BEEN THE BIGGEST, TOUGHEST, BRAVEST VAMPIRES.

RIGHT. COMPARED TO THE OTHER PRINCES, I AM A SLIGHT LITTLE WISP.

UMM...

GU (HRRG)

WHAT DO YOU THINK, DARREN?

THEY'RE NOT VERY BIG BICEPS.

TON (TAP)

I'M THE FIRST TO BE NOMINATED BECAUSE OF *THIS.*

...ARE A SIGN OF TRUST.

THESE SCARS ON MY CHEEK...

I'M THE FIRST VAMPIRE SINCE THE SIGNING OF THE PEACE TREATY TO SEEK AN UNDERSTANDING WITH THE VAMPANEZE.

WHEN KURDA HOLDS FULL POWER, THE NEGOTIATIONS WILL BE MUCH SMOOTHER.

THAT IS WHY HE IS BEING INVESTED.

A MAJORITY OF THE GENERALS THINK IT IS TIME WE WERE REUNITED WITH THE VAMPANEZE.

...OF COURSE! THE SIGN THAT MURLOUGH MARKED ON HIS PREY!

I FEAR THE POSSIBILITY THAT THE VAMPANEZE COULD USE YOU...

I THINK THAT YOU ARE PUSHING THINGS MUCH TOO FAST FOR MY LIKING.

YOU DON'T AGREE WITH IT, LARTEN?

NIKO. (GRIN)

I THINK IT'S WRONG TO KILL HUMANS ...

I DON'T KNOW IF WE SHOULD STRIKE A DEAL WITH THEM...

IS IT TIME FOR A CHANGE—FOR VAMPIRES TO ACCEPT THEIR WAYWARD BRETHREN?

WHAT DO *YOU* THINK, DARREN?

...BUT IF YOU COULD PERSUADE THE VAMPANEZE TO STOP KILLING...

...IT MIGHT BE A GOOD THING.

I'D LIKE THAT!

WE MUST HAVE A PROPER CHAT LATER, DARREN.

I GUESS I'LL FIND OUT THE TRUTH OF THE MESSAGE WHEN I REPORT TO THE HALL OF PRINCES.

ANYWAY, I CAN'T STAY HIDDEN FOREVER.

KURDA.

GACHA CLICKS

LARTEN.

TA (CHOP)

FUN CHRRMD

PEACEFUL COEXISTENCE WITH THE VAMPANEZE!

I LIKE HIM.

KURDA'S NICE.

AHA!

IT'S THE FOURTH DAY SINCE I ARRIVED AT VAMPIRE MOUNTAIN.

HARKAT'S STILL LOCKED UP IN THE HALL OF PRINCES, UNDERGOING QUESTIONING. I'M WORRIED FOR HIM.

EVEN SEBA WAS UNABLE TO HIDE HIS ANXIETY OVER HARKAT'S MESSAGE.

...SO WE ONLY SEE HIM WHEN HE COMES BACK FOR SLEEP.

THANKS, SEBA.

GAVNER HAS PLENTY OF GENERAL BUSINESS TO ATTEND TO...

"GORO (ROLL)"

THE UPROAR OVER THE MESSAGE REFUSES TO DIE DOWN.

"THE NIGHT OF THE VAMPANEZE LORD IS AT HAND..."

CHAPTER 31:
THE HALL OF DEATH

SURELY YOU DO NOT MEAN TO BELITTLE YOUR OWN WORK WITH THE SPEAR!

WHY, I CAN STILL SEE IT FLASHING BEFORE MY EYES!

AND THE WAY YOU FOUGHT IN THAT BATTLE, LARTEN!

GAYA

GAYA (MURMUR)

BWA

HA HA

GREETINGS, DARREN.

SU (SHH)

KURDA SMAHLT!

GAYA

REALLY?

GAYA (MURMUR)

I THOUGHT I MIGHT TAKE YOU ON A TOUR OF THE HALLS.

THINGS ARE CALMING DOWN AT LAST, AND I HAVE A FEW FREE HOURS.

YOU CAN TAG ALONG IF YOU WANT, LARTEN.

YOU DO THE BOY A GREAT HONOUR.

A MAN OF YOUR EMINENCE, ACTING AS GUIDE SO CLOSE TO YOUR INVESTITURE.

READY, DARREN?

READY!

FUN (CHRRM)

NO THANK YOU.

OKAY, YOUR LOSS.

YOU DIDN'T SEE MANY ANIMALS AROUND THE MOUNTAIN, DID YOU?

THAT'S WHY WE RAISE OUR OWN LIVESTOCK WITHIN THE MOUNTAIN FOR MEAT AND MILK.

THESE ARE THE KITCHENS.

THE COOKS WORK IN SHIFTS AROUND THE CLOCK WHEN THE COUNCIL IS IN SESSION.

I'VE BEEN WORKING AT IT FOR DECADES, BUT IT'S EVEN HARDER THAN YOU MIGHT THINK.

EACH TIME I HAVE THE LUXURY OF EXPLORING, I NOTICE OLD TUNNELS THAT HAVE COLLAPSED, AND NEW ONES THAT HAVE OPENED UP...

THEY CRISS-CROSS THE ENTIRE MOUNTAIN, YOU SEE.

SOME OF THE TUNNELS ARE WELL MAINTAINED, AND SOME AREN'T.

...THEY'VE MOSTLY BEEN LEFT ALONE FOR THOUSANDS OF YEARS.

ASIDE FROM THE ONES THAT CONNECT THE MAJOR HALLS...

...BUT ONE OF MY HOBBIES IS MAPMAKING. I WANT TO MAKE AN ACCURATE MAP OF VAMPIRE MOUNTAIN.

YOU MIGHT LAUGH AT THIS CONFESSION...

THE OTHER VAMPIRES JUST FIND IT SILLY.

YOU'RE ABOUT THE ONLY PERSON TO EVER SAY THAT.

YOU DO?

THAT'S NOT STRANGE. I THINK IT'S INTERESTING!

THERE ARE HARDLY ANY WHO SAY THAT.

PERHAPS AFTER ALL THE TIME WE SPEND SLEEPING IN COFFINS, WE'VE HAD ENOUGH.

WHAT IF THEY DON'T WANT TO BE CREMATED?

THIS IS WHERE WE CREMATE THE VAMPIRES WHO HAVE DIED IN THE MOUNTAIN.

THE HALL OF CREMATION.

WHAT THIS

THERE'S A CAVE FOR THAT CALLED THE HALL OF FINAL VOYAGE, ALTHOUGH IT'S NEVER USED NOW.

HYUGOO (SWOOOSH)

NOT SO LONG AGO, WE'D LOWER THE DEAD INTO AN UNDERGROUND STREAM AND LET THEM WASH AWAY...

EXACTLY! I'LL TAKE YOU THERE SOMEDAY.

BE-CAUSE OF YOUR MAPS!

ASIDE FROM SEBA AND THE OTHER PRINCES, I'M THE ONLY ONE WHO COULD SHOW YOU THE WAY THERE.

NI CGRIN

PATAN
(THUMP)

OH!

KOSO
(SNEAK)

THOSE AREN'T VAMPIRES...

...ARE THEY?

...SETTING THE SPIRIT OF THE DEAD VAMPIRE FREE.

THE DUST IS THEN THROWN TO THE WINDS AROUND VAMPIRE MOUNTAIN...

WE USE THEM TO CRUSH THE BONES IN THE PESTLES.

OVER HERE, DARREN! COME!

KURDA, WHO WAS—

WHAT ARE THE STICKS FOR?

THIS IS THE CREMATION PIT.

AREN'T YOU WORRIED ABOUT MR. TINY'S MESSAGE, KURDA?

I'D BE LYING IF I SAID I WASN'T CONCERNED...

...BUT I'M HONESTLY TOO BUSY ALREADY WITH WHAT'S AHEAD.

SU (SHH)

BESIDES, IF WE CAN BROKER A PEACE WITH THE VAMPANEZE, THERE WON'T **BE** A WAR TO WORRY ABOUT.

AS LONG AS I DO MY JOB, WE'LL BE FINE!

GOOD POINT.

JUST A MOMENT.

YOU DON'T WANT TO GO IN THERE.

IT'S NOT A VERY PLEAS- ANT PLACE...

WHAT IS IT?

IT'S THE CUSTOM WE PERFORM AS WE PASS THIS HALL.

WHAT WAS THAT?

CAN I?

YOU WANT TO GO IN?

DEATH!

THE HALL OF DEATH.

ALL RIGHT, BUT ONLY FOR A MOMENT ...

!!!

OVER HERE, DARREN.

IT LOOKS LIKE JUST A NORMAL ROOM ...

THERE'S ANOTHER ONE...

OVER AND OVER...

THE VAMPIRE TO BE EXECUTED IS PUT INTO A CAGE AND LOWERED ONTO THE SPIKES UNTIL HE IS DEAD.

THIS IS WHERE THE LEGEND OF THE STAKE THROUGH THE HEART ORIGINATED.

GIRA (GLINT)

WHO DO THEY KILL HERE?

B-BUT *WHY?*

SFX: BURU (SHIVER)

WE WOULD RATHER FACE DEATH ON OUR FEET THAN LET OUR FRIENDS LOOK AFTER US IN OLD AGE.

THOSE WHO LACK THE STRENGTH TO DIE ON THEIR FEET ASK TO COME HERE.

USUALLY THE OLD OR CRIPPLED VAMPIRES.

NO. THEY LOOK DEATH IN THE EYE, TO SHOW THEY ARE PROUD AND NOT AFRAID.

DO YOU GIVE THEM BLIND-FOLDS?

THE TREACH-EROUS TOO.

THERE HAVE ONLY BEEN SIX TRAITORS EXECUTED HERE THROUGHOUT OUR HISTORY.

THESE ARE THE HALLS OF SPORT.

WAA
(RAHHH)

BUSHU
(BUSHH)

GA
(WHACK)

KA
(SNIK)

WHY DON'T THEY WEAR PROTECTIVE CLOTHING IF THEY'RE USING REAL WEAPONS?

HE LOST AN EYE... AND HE'S LAUGHING...

SFX: ZOZO (SHIVER)

SU DD (SWISH)

YOU'RE WRONG, KURDA! IT'S BECAUSE IT IS COWARDLY!

WE'D RATHER DIE THAN SUFFER THE SHAME OF DONNING ARMOUR!

ARMOUR IS VIRTUALLY USELESS AGAINST SUCH MIGHT.

THEY USED TO IN THE PAST, BUT YOU KNOW THE SPEED AND STRENGTH OF A VAMPIRE.

GAYA

GAYA (MURMUR)

THE DUELS EVOLVED TO FAVOUR EASE OF MOVEMENT RATHER THAN PRO-TECTION.

GAYA

SFX: UOOO (RAHHH) / FU (HEH) FU FU

... VANEZ.

I WISH YOU'D TAKE A MORE LOGICAL VIEW OF THE SITUATION...

THERE ARE TIMES WHEN I DON'T KNOW MY OWN PEOPLE AT ALL...

HEH! NOT HALF BAD!

DARREN, THIS IS VANEZ BLANE, A GAMES MASTER.

ZA (ZSHH)

YO!

I-IS THAT HOW YOU LOST YOUR EYE...?

GAYA (MURMUR)

GAYA

DID THAT MATCH SCARE YOU?

I JUST WATCH OVER THE HALL TO MAKE SURE PEOPLE CAN GET INJURED OR KILLED ANY WAY THEY WANT!

IT'S A FANCY TITLE, BUT IT DOESN'T MEAN MUCH.

WHAT'S A GAMES MASTER?

A LION?

NO, I LOST MINE IN A FIGHT WITH A LION!

HA HA HA

HAVE YOU EVER HEARD OF A VAMPIRE WHO DIDN'T LIKE BLOOD?

KURDA WAS FAST AS AN EEL, AND WIRY, BUT HE HATED GETTING HIS HANDS BLOODY.

HA HA HA...

VANEZ!

SHEESH...

MOST OF THE GENERALS HAVE STUDIED UNDER HIM, MYSELF INCLUDED.

VANEZ IS ONE OF OUR MOST VALUED INSTRUCTORS. HE TRAINS VAMPIRES TO FIGHT.

WE USE ALL OF THEM IN THE DUELS HERE.

ISN'T THIS A SIGHT, DARREN?

ZURA (CLONG)

DOSASA (THWOMP)

WAA (RAHH)

WE ONLY FIGHT HAND TO HAND. NO MISSILE WEAPONS.

THERE ARE NO GUNS OR BOWS AND ARROWS.

ANY VAMPIRE WHO RESORTS TO A GUN OR BOW WOULD BE HELD IN CONTEMPT FOR THE REST OF HIS LIFE.

IT'S A SACRED RULE TO US—AND THE VAMPANEZE AS WELL.

FUN
(HMPH)

HELLO, I'M DARREN SHAN...

SU
(SHH)

AND SHE RESPECTS PRECIOUS FEW OF US...

ARRA DOESN'T SHAKE THE HANDS OF THOSE SHE DOESN'T RESPECT.

...BUT I WILL NEVER SHAKE YOUR HAND.

WHEN YOU BECOME PRINCE, I WILL BOW TO YOU AND DO YOUR BIDDING...

I WILL NEVER SHAKE THE HAND OF ONE WHO DOES NOT FIGHT.

STILL REFUSING TO SHAKE HANDS WITH *ME*, ARRA?

I DIDN'T VOTE FOR YOU EITHER.

I DON'T THINK ARRA VOTED FOR ME IN THE ELECTION...

YOU CAN'T BE SERIOUS, VANEZ!

ME?

DARREN, HOW WOULD YOU LIKE TO TRY OUT THE BARS WITH ARRA?

VANEZ!

HUH?

IT WILL BE A NOVEL EXPERIENCE.

ANY OBJECTIONS TO FIGHTING A SMALLER OPPONENT?

I WILL FACE ANY VAMPIRE WHO CHALLENGES ME, WITH ALL MY MIGHT, REGARDLESS OF HIS SIZE.

BUT...

...ONLY IF HE HAS THE COURAGE.

MERA CHRMPHD

WELL STATED, BOY! HERE YOU GO!

...WAIT, YOU'RE *ACCEPTING* THE DUEL?

THAT'S RIGHT, DON'T LISTEN TO—

NO. I ACCEPT THE FIGHT!

DON'T HEED HER CHALLENGE, DARREN!

STOP THEM, VANEZ!

SFX: FUN (HMPH)

AND IF I WIN, WILL YOU SHAKE MY HAND?

PASHI (SNATCH)

YOU OUGHT TO LEARN A LESSON ABOUT HOW TO SPEAK TO YOUR ELDERS, BOY...

130

CHAPTER 32:
THE FIRST DUEL

WAA
(RAHH)

UO
(WHOO)

I'LL HAVE THAT HANDSHAKE, WHETHER SHE LIKES IT OR NOT!!

I'M NOT GOING TO BACK DOWN AFTER SHE HUMILIATED ME!

STOP ENCOURAGING HIM! THIS IS MAD!

THERE'S NO WAY HE CAN HANDLE ARRA!

UOO (WHOOA)

WAA (RAHHH)

LISTEN UP, DARREN.

ARRA HASN'T LOST A MATCH ON THE BARS IN ELEVEN YEARS, DARREN!

YOU CAN STILL QUIT NOW, WHILE THERE'S TIME!

KNOCK YOUR OPPONENT OFF THE BARS ONTO THE GROUND.

THE RULES ARE SIMPLE:

...SO IN YOUR CASE, USE SHORT JABS AND KEEP YOUR DISTANCE. TRY TO STRIKE WHEN YOU SEE AN OPENING.

IT WON'T BE EASY TO BEAT ARRA...

FACE EACH OTHER!

NOW FIGHT!!

PAN (CLAP)

DARREN...

ALL THE MORE WORTH TRYING.

I DIDN'T KNOW SHE WAS THAT TOUGH...

LET'S START WITH A LITTLE GREETING ...

SUSUSU (SSLIP)

HOW MUCH OF THIS IS BECAUSE OF MY VAMPIRE BLOOD?

HOW MUCH CAN I DO ON MY OWN?

I WANT TO TEST MYSELF TOO.

HERE SHE COMES!

HYU (ZIP)

GA (THUK)

KA (TAK)

KA

SHE'S FAST!

3

GURU (SPIN)

SHE CALLS THIS...

BIRI (THROB)

BIRI

...A GREET-ING?

BACHII (ZPOWW)

I'M CALL-ING AN END TO THIS!

ARE YOU OUT TO KILL HIM, ARRA?

GAKU (SLUMP)

NO!

I WILL STAND DOWN.

AS YOU WISH.

WHA
...?!

DOBA
(OBONK!)

NOW!

GURUN
(SPIN)

BASHI
(THWAK)

UO
(OOOH)

AHH! DARREN
MANAGED TO
STRIKE ARRA
A CLEAN
BLOW!

...YOU CAN STRAP ME INTO A CAGE IN THE HALL OF DEATH AND DROP ME ON THE STAKES!

BETTER WATCH YOURSELF, ARRA. IF THE BOY BEATS YOU...

THAT WAS THE WEAKEST BLOW I'VE EVER FELT!

WHAT?

GI
(GLARE)

SHA
(HOP)

SHA

SHA

I'M THE ONE WHO HAS TO BE CAREFUL!

THAT LAST ONE WAS JUST A LUCKY SHOT.

I WON'T STAND A CHANCE IF WE KEEP TRADING BLOWS!

I'VE GOT TO TAKE VANEZ'S ADVICE AND KEEP MY DISTANCE UNTIL I CAN STRIKE!

BA
(LEAP)

OH,
HELL!

SUSUSU
(SSSK)

TRAPPED IN
A CORNER!
SHE OUTMA-
NOEUVRED
ME....

8

DOBACHI
(THWACK)

NO WAY!
HOW DID
SHE GET
PAST ME?

GUN
(GRAB)

KARAN
(CLANG)

BATA
(FLOP)

PORO
(DROP)

DARREN!

GU
(RGH)

LET HIM FIGHT.

DON'T DISGRACE HIM IN FRONT OF ALL THESE VAMPIRES, KURDA!

GORO
(ROLL)

IT DID NOT TAKE MUCH POWER FOR ME TO...

...BUT STILL JUST A HALF-VAMPIRE.

YOU WERE A TENACIOUS OPPONENT...

GU
(SHOVE)

REACH!

BA
(WHOOSH)

PASHI
(SNAG)

GA
(WHUD)

LOOKS LIKE I WIN!

GURI
(HRRG)

BA
(SWOOSH)

GASHU!
(SNAG)

AH!

PACHI
(CLAP)

PACHI

UOOOO
(WHOAAA)

SHA

SHA
(ZWIP)

TA
(TEK)

OOO
(OOOH!)

ARRA STOLE THE STAFF BACK FROM HIM!

AAH!

BESHA
(FLOP)

GUI
(TUG)

WOULD YOU LIKE A REPLACEMENT?

HOW ABOUT IT, *BOY?*

HE CAN'T DEFEND HIM-SELF WITH HIS BARE HANDS! IT'S NOT FAIR!

SHE WANTS ME TO SURREN-DER THE FIGHT...

...IN WHICH CASE...

GUGU
(UGHH)

......

N O !!!

WELL FOUGHT, DARREN!

ARRA HAS WON THIS...

THERE WILL BE NO SHAME IN QUITTING NOW!

NO QUIT-TING!!

I WON'T GET OFF THESE BARS TILL I'M KNOCKED OFF!!

...IT'S GOING TO HURT.

KA (WHAK)

BUT...

I SEE.

VERY WELL...

DO DO DO DO DO (WHAM)

HYU (SWISH)

THE POOR CHILD DOESN'T KNOW WHETHER HE'S COMING OR GOING!

BWA HA HA HA HA HA HA

HOW MUCH FARTHER TO VAMPIRE MOUNTAIN?

UGH... WHERE AM I?

ZAWA (MURMUR)

ZAWA

DARREN...

WAKE UP, DARREN...

DARREN!

ARRA! WHERE'S ARRA?

...OH! WAIT!

AND IF I DON'T?

::SHAKE!

COME...

SHAKE!

ONE GOOD FIGHT DOESN'T MAKE YOU A WARRIOR.

YORO (LURCH)

...AND FIGHT YOU TILL YOU DO!

I'LL GET BACK UP ON THE BARS...

......

POWER TO YOU, DARREN SHAN.

POW-ER.

148

CHAPTER 33:
THE HALL
OF PRINCES

...TWO NIGHTS AFTER MY ENCOUNTER WITH ARRA SAILS...

...MR. CREPSLEY AND I WERE CALLED BEFORE THE VAMPIRE PRINCES.

OUCH! THAT HURTS...

EVEN *I* WOULD HESITATE AT GOING ONE-ON-ONE WITH HER.

I CANNOT BELIEVE YOU WERE FOOLISH ENOUGH TO CHALLENGE ARRA SAILS.

YOU SOUND LIKE KURDA.

YOU COULD HAVE BEEN SERIOUSLY INJURED.

STUPIDITY AND BRAVERY ARE NOT THE SAME THING.

GUESS THAT MEANS I'M BRAVER THAN YOU.

.....BUT YOU ARE IMPOSSIBLE TO TALK TO.

DO NOT COMPARE ME TO HIM.

PA (PAT)

PA

NOW FINISH DRESSING AND MAKE YOURSELF PRESENTABLE.

WE MUST NOT KEEP THE PRINCES WAITING.

HEH HEH.

...WHO COULD KNOCK THE STAFF OUT OF ARRA'S HANDS.

THERE ARE VERY FEW VAMPIRES ALIVE...

BASA (FLAP)

IT'S ALL VERY IMPRESSIVE.

THIS IS THE ONLY HALLWAY TO IT.

THE HALL OF PRINCES IS THE HIGHEST LOCATION INSIDE THE MOUNTAIN.

HOW FAR DOES THIS GO?

I WILL TAKE YOUR FOOTWEAR.

HERE WE ARE.

WEAPONS OF ALL KINDS ARE FORBIDDEN IN THE HALL.

ONE COULD SLIP A DAGGER IN A SHOE, IF HE FELT LIKE IT.

WHY?

THEY ARE. THIS IS FOR TRADITION'S SAKE MORE THAN ANYTHING ELSE.

I THOUGHT THE PRINCES WERE RESPECTED AND OBEYED BY ALL VAMPIRES.

WHY ALL THE SECURITY?

...THE HALL OF PRINCES.

THIS IS THE CORE OF VAMPIRE MOUNTAIN...

WHAT'S THAT...? IT'S GLOWING.

DOKLIN
(THUMP)

IT IS THE TOUGHEST MATERIAL KNOWN TO MAN OR VAMPIRE.

NOTHING CAN PENETRATE ITS WALLS... NO TOOL, EXPLOSIVE OR ACID.

DOKLIN

DOKLIN

WHERE DID IT COME FROM?

PLACE YOUR HANDS ON IT.

I DON'T SEE ANY CRACKS OR JOINTS.

WHAT'S IT MADE OF—ROCK, MARBLE, IRON?

AND IT THROBS!

OH! IT'S WARM!

WE DO NOT KNOW WHAT THE MATERIAL IS, OR HOW IT WAS BUILT.

IF ANYTHING, BOTH ANSWERS PROBABLY INVOLVE MAGIC.

...MR. TINY PRESENTED US WITH THIS DOME AND THE STONE OF BLOOD.

CENTURIES AGO, AFTER THE VAMPANEZE BROKE AWAY FROM THE VAMPIRES ...

PAA
(GLOW)

THE ENTIRE STRUCTURE IS GLOWING!

IT'S EVEN BRIGHTER INSIDE...

ZAWA

ZAWA
(MURMUR)

GAWA

GAWA
(MURMUR)

YOU SEE THE RED STONE BEHIND THE PRINCES?

THAT STONE? IT JUST LOOKS LIKE COLOURED GLASS...

THAT IS THE STONE OF BLOOD—THE KEY TO THE LONGEVITY OF THE VAMPIRE RACE ITSELF.

...LINKING HIM TO THE MENTAL COLLECTIVE OF THE CLAN FOR-EVER.

WHEN A VAMPIRE IS ACCEPTED, HE GIVES HIS OWN NAME AND BLOOD TO THE STONE...

FIRST, TO REGISTER A NEW VAMPIRE TO THE FOLD.

THE STONE SERVES FOUR PURPOSES, BROADLY SPEAKING.

ZAWA

ZAWA

YOU KNOW HOW VAMPIRES CAN MENTALLY SEARCH FOR THOSE THEY HAVE BONDED WITH?

MENTAL COLLECTIVE?

...THAT WOULD BE THE SECOND USE OF THE STONE OF BLOOD.

WELL, THE STONE BINDS US ALL MENTALLY. AND IF YOU WANTED TO FIND SOMEONE WHOM YOU HAVE NOT BONDED WITH...

ONE VAMPIRE TRACKS THE TARGET'S LO-CATION WITH THE STONE...

BUT IT REQUIRES TRIANGU-LATION.

...AND RELAYS THE INFORMA-TION MENTALLY TO THE VAMPIRE ON THE CHASE, EVEN AS THE TARGET MOVES.

TARGET

ANYONE, AS LONG AS THEY HAVE IDENTIFIED THEM-SELVES TO THE STONE.

EVEN IF THEY DIDN'T WANT TO BE FOUND?

WHAT IF THE VAMPANEZE GOT THEIR HANDS ON IT, AND...

ISN'T THE STONE DANGEROUS THEN?

ANYONE WITH THE ABILITY TO SEARCH MENTALLY.

CAN ANYONE USE THE STONE OF BLOOD TO FIND A VAMPIRE?

GAYA ガヤ

GAYA (MURMUR) ガヤ

HMMM...

...UNTIL THE VAMPIRE RACE HAD COME TO AN END.

IF THAT WERE TO PASS, THEY WOULD HUNT US DOWN ONE BY ONE...

PASA (FLAP)

パサ

YOUR REASONING IS IMPRESSIVE, MASTER SHAN.

THIS IS THE THIRD USE OF THE STONE OF BLOOD.

IT ALSO SERVES AS THE SOURCE OF POWER FOR THE HALL OF PRINCES.

THERE ARE REASONS NOT TO ATTEMPT IT, NOT LEAST OF WHICH IS ITS INDE-STRUCTIBLE NATURE.

WOULDN'T IT BE BETTER JUST TO BREAK THE STONE?

...IS THE FOURTH AND FINAL USE.

BUT MOST IMPOR-TANT OF ALL...

156

IT IS OUR ONLY HOPE TO COMBAT THE VAMPANEZE LORD OF MR. TINY'S PROPHECY.

THE STONE OF BLOOD IS THE VERY SYMBOL OF VAMPIRE ORDER AND UNITY.

...SO WE CANNOT BLITHELY IGNORE HIS PROPHECY.

IT WAS MR. TINY WHO INFUSED THE STONE WITH POWER...

NOW MORE THAN EVER, WE MUST PROTECT THE STONE.

AS LONG AS WE'VE GOT THE STONE OF BLOOD, THERE'S A CHANCE THAT VAMPIRES MIGHT RISE FROM THE ASHES...

IT'S GAVNER AND KURDA!

AND HARKAT!

DARREN, LARTEN!

SFX: ZAWA (MURMUR) ZAWA

158

THERE IS ONE MORE PRINCE WHO IS ABSENT, BUT THERE WILL ALWAYS BE AT LEAST ONE IN ATTENDANCE AT ALL TIMES.

DARREN, THOSE ARE OUR LEADERS, THE VAMPIRE PRINCES.

FINALLY, THERE IS ARROW.

...BUT RETURNED TO US WHEN SHE WAS MURDERED BY A VAM-PANEZE. HE IS AT THE FOREFRONT OF ANTI-VAMPANEZE SENTIMENT.

HE MARRIED A HUMAN WOMAN IN THE PAST, LEAVING OUR KIND ...

IN THE CENTRE IS PARIS SKYLE.

HE IS THE OLDEST LIVING VAMPIRE AT OVER 800 YEARS...

...AND A LIVING LEGEND.

ON OUR RIGHT IS MIKA VER LETH.

HE IS THE YOUNGEST OF THE CURRENT PRINCES AT 270 YEARS OF AGE AND IS A FIERCE WARRIOR.

TIME TO GO.

DARREN SHAN, TO THE FRONT!

LARTEN CREPSLEY!

GATA (THUMP)

AT ONCE!

I DID NOT THINK I WOULD LOOK UPON YOUR FACE AGAIN.

IT IS GOOD TO SEE YOU, LARTEN.

ZA (BOW)

HE'S JUST A *BOY!* WHAT POSSESSED YOU TO...

... MIKA.

LET US NOT SPEAK RASHLY OF LARTEN...

GAVNER PURL HAS SPOKEN APPROVINGLY OF HIM.

THIS MUST BE YOUR ASSISTANT, DARREN SHAN.

HEH-HEH

I THOUGHT IT WAS TOO HANDSOME A FACE TO HIDE!

... DIRECTLY FROM YOUR OWN MOUTH, LARTEN.

I WISH TO HEAR YOUR REASONS FOR BLOODING YOUNG DARREN...

THERE IS BUT ONE REASON WE HAVE CALLED YOU HERE TODAY.

KNOWING YOU, THERE MUST HAVE BEEN GOOD REASON.

WHY DID YOU BREAK OUR TRADITION?

I HAVE...

...NO VALID REASON.

DOYO (BUZZ)

WE MUST HAVE QUIET!

THERE WILL BE QUIET IN THE HALL!

ZAWA (MURMUR)

IS THAT ALL YOU HAVE TO SAY FOR YOURSELF, LARTEN!?

NO.

YOU WOULD NOT BLOOD A BOY OUT OF SIMPLE WHIMSY.

COME, LARTEN, DO NOT PLAY GAMES.

THERE IS NO ACCEPTABLE EXCUSE THAT I CAN GIVE FOR MY ACTIONS.

YET I DID. I WENT AGAINST ALL REASON WHEN I BLOODED DARREN AND MADE HIM A HALF-VAMPIRE.

...MAY I INTERVENE ON MY FRIEND'S BEHALF?

GATA (THUMP)

MY PRINCES...

BE SILENT, DARREN!

NO! MR. CREPSLEY ONLY DID IT BECAUSE—

I DON'T KNOW IF I CAN DO THAT...

WE WELCOME YOUR INPUT, IF IT CAN CLEAR THINGS UP.

ドゥヨ DOYO (MURMUR)

DOYO

BY ALL MEANS, GAVNER, SPEAK.

...IS AN EXTRA-ORDINARY BOY!

BUT I'D LIKE TO NOTE THAT DARREN...

I'M SURE YOU HAVE HEARD OF HIS CONTEST WITH ARRA SAILS, AS WELL.

...AND FOUGHT A BEAR POISONED WITH VAM-PANEZE BLOOD ALONG THE WAY.

HE MADE THE TREK TO VAMPIRE MOUNTAIN— NO SMALL FEAT FOR ONE HIS AGE...

IT WILL SET A DANGEROUS PRECEDENT IF THE ACT OF BLOODING A YOUNG BOY IS ALLOWED TO PASS!

BUT THAT'S NOT THE POINT!

YOU WERE ONLY TWO YEARS OLD WHEN YOU WERE BLOODED, WEREN'T YOU, SIRE?

I BE-LIEVE HE HAS THE MAKINGS OF A FINE VAMPIRE.

HE IS BRIGHT AND BRAVE, WILY AND HONEST.

WE MUST ADDRESS THE ISSUE OF LARTEN'S ACTIONS.

MIKA IS RIGHT.

THE FAULT IS MINE, AND I ALONE SHOULD BE PUNISHED, BY EXECUTION IF NECESSARY.

I DO NOT SEEK FORGIVENESS.

I MERELY ASK THAT NO REPRISALS BE TAKEN AGAINST DARREN.

IT WOULD BE WRONG OF US TO IGNORE THE PRECEDENT THIS WOULD SET.

THEY SPEAK THE TRUTH, LARTEN.

...AND DIE MEETING IT IF I MUST.

IF YOU DECIDE I MUST BE TESTED, I WILL RISE TO ANY CHALLENGE YOU CARE TO SET...

THEY CAN'T KILL YOU BECAUSE OF *ME*!

SHIIIN (SHHHH)

DRAGGING YOUR GOOD NAME THROUGH THE MUCK IS NOT OUR INTENTION.

NONE OF US WISHES TO DO THAT.

YOUR GOOD STANDING IS NOT IN QUESTION, NOR WILL IT EVER BE.

HOWEVER...

WE RESERVE CHALLENGES FOR THOSE WHO HAVE NOT PROVEN THEMSELVES IN BATTLE.

SU
(POINT)

...BUT WHETHER HE HAS THE COURAGE AND SKILLS EXPECTED OF A TRUE VAMPIRE.

THE QUESTION IS NOT OF THE BOY'S AGE OR INEXPERIENCE...

THERE *IS* A WAY TO RESOLVE THIS WITHOUT KILLING OUR OLD FRIEND OR SOILING HIS GOOD NAME.

THE TALK OF CHALLENGES GAVE ME AN IDEA.

PERHAPS...

ZAWA
(MURMUR)

LET'S SET A CHALLENGE FOR THE *BOY!*

BI
(JAB)

166

THE TRIALS OF INITIATION

ZAWA

ZAWA (MURMUR)

YOU SAID YOU DIDN'T WANT HIM TO BE *PUNISHED.*

A CHALLENGE IS NOT A PUNISHMENT.

A CHALLENGE FOR THE BOY...

YES ...

NOT QUITE.

I SAID I DID NOT WANT TO BRING DARREN INTO THIS ...

...YOUR DECISION TO BLOOD HIM WILL BE ACCEPTED.

IF THE BOY PROVES HIMSELF IN A TEST...

IT IS FAIR, LARTEN.

ARE YOU PREPARED TO PROVE YOURSELF TO THE CLAN AND CLEAR OUR NAMES?

THE DISHONOUR WILL BE *HIS* IF HE FAILS.

AND NO MORE WILL NEED BE SAID ABOUT IT.

I WILL NOT FORCE A CHALLENGE ON HIM.

VERY WELL. BUT THE DECISION IS DARREN'S, NOT MINE.

...WHAT SORT OF A CHALLENGE ARE WE TALKING ABOUT, EXACTLY?

UM...

NO!!!

DA

DA (STOMP)

WHICH LEAVES ONLY...

AND A QUEST WOULD TAKE TOO LONG.

IT WOULD BE UNFAIR TO PIT YOU IN BATTLE AGAINST ONE OF OUR WARRIORS.

A HALF-VAMPIRE IS NO MATCH FOR A GENERAL.

A GOOD QUES-TION.

KURDA!

BA (LEAP)

I WILL NOT STAND FOR THIS!!!

DARREN...

IF YOU INSIST ON TESTING HIM, LET HIM WAIT TILL HE IS OLDER!

THE BOY ISN'T READY FOR THE TRIALS!

...SO DON'T ACT LIKE ONE!

GU (URGH)

YOU'RE NOT A PRINCE YET...

THERE WILL BE NO WAIT-ING!

WE WIELD THE AUTHORITY HERE, KURDA SMAHLT!

THE TRIALS OF INITIATION ARE TESTS FOR VAMPIRES WHO WISH TO BECOME GENERALS.

YOU HAVE.

MY APOLOGIES FOR SPEAKING OUT OF TURN, SIRE.

HAVE I THE PERMISSION OF THE PRINCES TO SPEAK?

THE TRIALS OF INITIATION ...

THEY WERE NOT DESIGNED FOR A HALF-VAMPIRE CHILD. IT WOULD NOT BE FAIR.

YOU'LL BE SIGNING YOUR DEATH WARRANT IF YOU SAY YES.

YOU MUSTN'T AGREE TO THIS, DARREN.

THE VAMPIRE IS NOT TOLD OF THEIR TASK UNTIL JUST BEFOREHAND.

THE TESTS ARE PICKED AT RANDOM AND ARE WIDELY VARIED.

IT WILL INVOLVE FIVE ACTS OF PHYSICAL COURAGE.

SOME ARE HARDER THAN OTHERS, BUT NONE IS EASY.

OR TO DODGE A STEADY CASCADE OF FALLING BOULDERS.

IT MIGHT BE TO DIVE INTO A DEEP POOL TO RETRIEVE A MEDALLION.

I DIS-AGREE.

THEY'RE FOR FULL VAMPIRES, DARREN.

YOU AREN'T STRONG, QUICK OR EXPERIENCED ENOUGH FOR THE TRIALS OF INITIATION.

ARROW?

I SAY IT'S THE TRIALS.

LET'S VOTE ON IT.

I WOULD NOT LET AN ASSISTANT STEP FORWARD IF I THOUGHT HE WOULD BE OUT OF HIS DEPTH.

DARREN *IS* CAPABLE OF PASSING THE TRIALS.

PARIS?

I AGREE. THE TRIALS.

I FEAR YOUR OPTIMISM MAY BE MIS-PLACED.

HMM... KURDA DOES HAVE A POINT, LARTEN.

AH, EXCELLENT.

SU (RISE)

DOES ANYONE HAVE ANYTHING TO ADD?

WHAT DO THE GENERALS THINK?

SPEAK, GENERAL ARRA SAILS.

...HOW MUCH THAT MEANS TO ME.

THOSE WHO KNOW ME WILL ALSO KNOW...

I HAVE SHAKEN HIS HAND.

I HAVE FULL RESPECT FOR DARREN SHAN.

ARRA!

DARREN MUST PROVE HIMSELF TO ALL, NOT JUST ME.

BUT I AGREE WITH MY PRINCES.

I SPEAK FROM PERSONAL EXPERIENCE.

HAVING SAID THAT, I DON'T THINK DARREN WILL LET US DOWN.

WE HAVE NO PLACE FOR CHILDREN WHO NEED TO BE WET-NURSED AND TUCKED INTO THEIR COFFINS AT DAYBREAK.

A VAMPIRE WHO CANNOT PULL HIS OWN WEIGHT IS OF NO USE TO US.

I BELIEVE HE WILL PASS THE TRIALS AND PROVE HIMSELF.

TO DENY DARREN THE RIGHT OF TRIALS WOULD BE TO SHAME HIM!

AND THOSE WHO SAY OTHERWISE—THOSE WHO'D WRAP HIM IN BLANKETS—SHOULD NOT BE HEEDED!

BETTER TO DIE WITH PRIDE THAN LIVE IN SHAME.

......

NOBLE WORDS. WILL YOU REPEAT THEM AT HIS FUNERAL?

HOW MANY THINK DARREN SHOULD UNDERTAKE THE TRIALS OF INITIATION?

LET US PUT IT TO THE HALL.

YES, ARRA. I SEE YOUR POINT.

7" GU (RGH)

WHAT ABOUT *YOU*, DARREN?

ARE YOU PREPARED TO FACE THEM?

BA
BA
BA (WHLIP)
BA
BA

!!

MR. CREPSLEY...

FOLLOW YOUR HEART.

SFX: CHIRA (GLANCE)

SIMPLY DO AS YOU WILL, DARREN.

...I WOULD SHAME MR. CREPSLEY...

...AND BE SENT FROM VAMPIRE MOUNTAIN IN DISGRACE.

IF I REFUSE THE TRIALS...

MY SHAME...

...IS MR. CREPSLEY'S SHAME.

THE ASSISTANT'S SHAME...

...IS THE MASTER'S SHAME.

NO ONE IS AS STUBBORN AS HE IS.

I'VE BEEN AROUND HIM FOR EIGHT YEARS.

...HE'D TRY TO TAKE RESPONSIBILITY, EVEN IF IT MEANT HIS OWN DEATH.

AND KNOWING MR. CREPSLEY...

BUT RIGHT NOW HE'S MY ONLY REAL FAMILY.

MY MASTER AND TEACHER.

I'VE HATED HIM.

I'VE EVEN WISHED I COULD KILL HIM...

UH...

HOW ABOUT IT, DARREN? WILL YOU FACE DEATH JUST TO PROVE YOURSELF TO THESE FOOLS?

BUT...

NO.

UH...

RETURN TO THE HALL OF PRINCES TOMORROW.

THEN IT IS DECIDED!

PAN

PAN (CLAP)

YOU MAY LEAVE NOW AND REST.

WE SHALL DRAW THE FIRST TRIAL THEN.

WE WILL SPEAK LATER.

?

DARREN, YOU WERE...

YOU GO BACK WITH GAVNER AND HARKAT.

I MUST DISCUSS THE TALE OF MURLOUGH WITH THE PRINCES, DARREN.

GAYA (MURMUR)

GAYA

NO. NOTHING.

HEH HEH

ALL RIGHT.

DON'T EXAGGER-ATE THE DANGER. YOU'LL FRIGHT-EN HIM!

TRY TOUGH AS THE WALLS OF THE HALL OF PRINCES.

VERY.

HOW TOUGH *ARE* THESE TRIALS?

DARREN WILL BE OKAY...

I NEARLY FAILED THEM MYSELF AFTER YEARS OF PREPARA-TION.

BUT THE TRIALS ARE TRULY FORMI-DABLE...

WEREN'T YOU LISTENING, DARREN? DIDN'T YOU UNDERSTAND?

WHAT DO YOU MEAN?

I CAN DROP OUT IF IT GETS OVER MY HEAD, CAN'T I?

DON'T WORRY! IF I FAIL, I CAN ALWAYS TRY AGAIN!

THEY REALLY *ARE* TOUGH, HUH?

YEAH... THEY ARE.

I'LL PRETEND I'VE GOT A TWISTED ANKLE OR SOMETHING.

SO I'LL FAIL. I'LL THROW IN THE TOWEL IF THINGS GET HAIRY.

THE GENERALS WON'T LET YOU.

YOU MIGHT FAIL, BUT YOU CAN'T QUIT.

NOBODY WALKS AWAY DURING THE MIDDLE OF THE TRIALS OF INITIATION.

WHAT DON'T I UNDERSTAND?

AND NOW THERE IS NO GOING BACK!

WE SHOULD'VE EXPLAINED IT FULLY BEFORE HE COULD AGREE!

CHARNA'S GUTS! HE *DOESN'T* UNDERSTAND!

∴DEATH!!!

IN THE TRIALS, FAILURE ENTAILS ONE FATE ONLY...

∴AND...

BUT SHOULD YOU FAIL AND NOT DIE, YOU WILL BE TAKEN TO THE HALL OF DEATH, STRAPPED INTO A CAGE, HOISTED ABOVE A PIT...

MOST WHO FAIL DIE IN THE ATTEMPT.

DEATH...

...DROPPED ON THE STAKES UNTIL YOU ARE DEAD!

W-WHAT SHOULD I DO, HARKAT...?

WHAT... REALLY?

THE TRIALS WERE MY PROBLEM... MY DESTINY... NO ONE COULD HELP ME NOW...

IN THE DARK HALLS OF VAMPIRE MOUNTAIN, I WOULD HAVE TO FACE DEATH ALONE...

BUT OF COURSE HARKAT COULDN'T ANSWER THAT.

VAMPIRE MOUNTAIN - END

A QUICK GUIDE TO THE STORY OF THE CIRQUE DU FREAK MANGA VERSION

(SORT OF)!!

PART 4!!!

MY THEME THIS TIME IS "FOOD." I'M COMPOSING THIS AFTERWORD WHILE I FONDLY REMEMBER THE SCHOOL LIFE I LED BACK IN SCOTLAND.

THAT BAT BROTH SOUNDS LIKE IT MUST BE RATHER TASTY.

ズズズ...
ZUZUZU (SLURRP)

WHILE SIPPING MISO SOUP.

THERE ARE PLENTY OF TAKE-AWAY RESTAURANTS NEAR MY OFFICE, WHICH HELPS SAVE LOTS OF MY TIME.

ジョキ ジョキ
JOKI JOKI (CHIK)

DO YOU REMEMBER IN THE FIRST VOLUME OF CIRQUE DU MANGA WHEN STEVE HAD HIS PAPERS KEPT IN A LITTLE BOX?

(IF YOU HAVEN'T SEEN IT OR DON'T REMEMBER, CHECK OUT P.31 OF VOLUME 1!)

AS I MENTIONED AT THE END OF THE PREVIOUS VOLUME, I DID SPEND PART OF MY LIFE IN SCOTLAND.

WHEN YOU MENTION ENGLISH FOOD, THERE'S NO IGNORING THE OLD STANDARD OF FISH AND CHIPS.

THIS IS ACTUALLY A SCHOOL LUNCHBOX, WHICH ARE QUITE COMMON IN THE UNITED KINGDOM.

HUH? THIS?

THEY'RE MADE OF PLASTIC, AND EVEN SIMPLER THAN THE ONES YOU SEE IN THE MANGA.

DECORATED WITH YOUR FAVOURITE SUPERHERO, ROBOT, OR CARTOON.

HEADS MAN

186

NOW, NOW...

PLEASE!

THE IDEAL LUNCH BOX LINEUP! YOU DON'T NEED ANYTHING ELSE!!

I HAD FRIENDS OF MANY DIFFERENT TYPES IN SCHOOL, BUT EVERYONE'S LUNCH WAS ROUGHLY THE SAME.

AT FIRST, MY MUM PUT IN RICE BALLS AND OTHER JAPANESE FOOD, BUT I CAN VIVIDLY REMEMBER MYSELF CRYING AND BEGGING HER TO MAKE MY LUNCH THE SAME AS EVERYONE ELSE'S!

APPLE, ORANGE OR BANANA

PEANUT BUTTER SANDWICH, OR SOMETIMES JAM

THERMOS FILLED WITH JUICE

CRISPS OR A CHOCOLATE BAR

THE RIGHT WAY TO EAT IT IS TO SHARE THE LEGS WITH YOUR FRIENDS.

YOU COULD EVEN GET HUGE CANDY SNAKES AND SPIDERS IF YOU HAD THE MONEY.

MY FAVOURITES WERE THE MULTICOLOURED JELLYBEANS IN THE CLEAR PLASTIC CASES!

PICK OUT WHAT YOU LIKE AND HAVE THEM WEIGHED BEFORE YOU BUY

IF I HAD MONEY AFTER SCHOOL, I'D SPLURGE AT THE SWEET SHOP.

...I GOT THE FEELING THAT THE ENGLISH ENJOY SCARY THINGS EVEN MORE THAN THE JAPANESE DO.

SEEMS LIKE A LOT OF ENGLISH PEOPLE LIKE SPOOKY, EERIE STUFF.

BETWEEN ALL THE GIANT CANDY SPIDERS AND THE EXTRAVAGANT HALLOWEEN DECORATIONS...

AS THE FIRST VOLUME TO END WITHOUT A CLIMAX, IT'S VERY INTRIGUING TO WONDER WHAT WILL HAPPEN NEXT! WHERE WILL FATE TAKE DARREN NEXT? FIND OUT IN VOLUME 5!

NOT THE TRIALS...

SO THE MANGA VERSION OF CIRQUE DU FREAK HAS JUMPED HEADFIRST INTO THE "VAMPIRE MOUNTAIN" STORY ARC.

The End

THE SAGA OF DARREN SHAN ④
Vampire Mountain

Darren Shan
Takahiro Arai

Translation: Stephen Paul
Lettering: AndWorld Design
Art direction: Hitoshi SHIRAYAMA
Original cover design: Shigeru ANZAI + Bay Bridge Studio

Darren Shan Vol. 4
Text © 2007 Darren Shan, Artworks © 2007 Takahiro ARAI
All rights reserved
Original Japanese edition published in Japan in 2007
by Shogakukan Inc., Tokyo
Artwork reproduction rights in U.K. and The Commonwealth arranged
with Shogakukan Inc. through Tuttle-Mori Agency, Inc., Tokyo.

English translation © Darren Shan 2010

Published in Great Britain by Harper Collins *Children's Books* 2010
Harper Collins *Children's Books* is a division of HarperCollins *Publishers* Ltd
77-85 Fulham Palace Road, Hammersmith, London, W6 8JB

www.harpercollins.co.uk

ISBN: 978 0 00 733271 7

Printed and bound in Great Britain by Clays Ltd, St Ives plc

Mixed Sources
Product group from well-managed
forests and other controlled sources
www.fsc.org Cert no. SW-COC-1806
© 1996 Forest Stewardship Council
FSC

FSC is a non-profit international organisation established to promote the
responsible management of the world's forests. Products carrying the FSC
label are independently certified to assure consumers that they come
from forests that are managed to meet the social, economic and
ecological needs of present and future generations.

Find out more about HarperCollins and the environment at
www.harpercollins.co.uk/green

The Saga of Darren Shan novels are available now.
How many have you read?

C153866237